about the author

J.M. Kearns, PhD, is a writer of fiction and non-fiction who has at various times been a philosopher of perception, a crisis counselor and a music journalist. He brings to his writing the unique combination of a philosopher's analytical mind and a novelist's insight into emotions. His best-selling *Why Mr. Right Can't Find You* has been published in Canada, the U.S., the UK, Australia, China, and France. Embraced by readers and the press, it was featured on Oprah & Friends and in *OK! Magazine, Glamour, Cosmopolitan-UK, Maclean's, The Toronto Star*, and many others. His most recent book is *Shopping for Mr. Right*. J.M. Kearns grew up near Toronto, Canada, and now lives in Cape May, New Jersey, with his partner, Debra.

For more on Kearns and his writings, please visit **www.jmkearns. com**.

praise for J.M. Kearns' writing:

"If you've been on the lookout for ages but still haven't found The One, this is for you . . . you'll be in the arms of your true love in no time!"

— *OK! Magazine*

"Practical, encouraging and . . . optimistic . . . Kearns gently undermines the conventions and insecurities that keep [women] from actively and effectively seeking a mate, including self-defeating myths ("Serious relationships never begin in bars") and media-inspired body-image issues . . . Personal anecdotes round out this thorough, thoughtful and entirely upbeat dating guide."

— *Publishers Weekly*

"I review self-help books for a living and this is the best self-help book I've ever read."

— Julia McKinnell, Contributing Editor, *Maclean's*

"'I'm bringing the good news from the male side of the trenches,' said J. M. Kearns . . . 'To set the record straight and defend the much-maligned male gender, who I think have been distorted in the self-help literature for years.' Mr. Kearns said . . . men [have been] presented in . . . dating literature as a homogeneous block to be tricked, decoded and subdued by women. 'If you worry about what most men are looking for, you'll go wrong,' he said. 'These books tell women they must act in accordance with a prescribed set of rules that has nothing to do with how men actually think.'"

— *Globe & Mail*

"Unlike most such books, *Why Mr. Right Can't Find You* is funny, inspiring and quite practical. A new book aimed specifically at successful, real single women, it may be just the thing you need to find Mr. Right-for-you. And it's been known to help a few men find their Ms. Right."
— Carolyn Cooke in *The Now Newspaper*

"J.M. Kearns in his excellent new book *Why Mr. Right Can't Find You* . . . unlike other self-helps for the single woman, starts with the premise that there is nothing wrong with you. You do not need to be 'fixed.' Kearns . . . has a PhD in philosophy and has worked as a crisis counsellor . . . Whereas other how-tos portray men as unknowable aliens interested only in hard-to-get women, Kearns has a different take. A lot of men . . . he says, want a meaningful relationship. 'Contrary to the dating books,' he writes, 'if you get into a conversation with the right man you won't have a problem knowing what to say!'"
— Julia McKinnell, *Maclean's*

readers speak about J.M. Kearns' writings:

"The book of hope. I followed its advice straight to a great new man I met, and now I'm happily married to him!"

— Olivia D.

"This book makes you look at relationships from a completely different perspective. I approached someone through an avenue I had never thought of before (because Kearns helped me to see opportunities, and empowered me to do something about it) and we have been dating ever since. The difference about this relationship is that I didn't approach it with a sense of lack or deficiency. This is truly a new day and a new way for me!"

— Lorraine L.

"This book doesn't even deserve to be lumped in with all the other "Self Help" stuff: it's better than that. I was shocked to find an intelligent discussion of something people almost never speak intelligently about—preferring instead to believe in some pie-in-the-sky fantasy at the exact moment they're planning a life! I brought this book to my boyfriend when we'd only been going out a few weeks: we read it together, talked about it, went on a road trip to test it out, and basically used it as a roadmap to find true compatibility . . . at the same time we were falling in love. I highly recommend it for couples, not just singles, because it jump-starts those conversations and questions you need to figure out before you get all emotional and sappy. We now know things about each other we'd never thought to ask ourselves. Oddly enough, after you figure out you really can be best friends and great partners, all that dreamy love stuff is much deeper and more rewarding. Great book—and the little vignettes make it hilarious, too."

— Marguerite P.

"I was really impressed with the logical thought, the clarity and the easy, creative way J.M. Kearns has of leading the reader from one thought to another. It's not patronizing but it is infused with patience and insight. On top of all that wisdom and perception, it is great fun to read. If only I had read this several relationships ago!"

— Janet C.

"Remarkably honest . . . the only genuinely open account I've ever seen, of what goes through a man's mind when he interacts with a woman. As a man I can say . . . yes, that's exactly how it is."

— August C. Bourré on *techsploitation.com*

"This book does even more than it thinks it's doing—it's good for men too! After reading it I became very aware that you can't just let 'sightings' pass you by. You have to be willing to take chances. J.M. Kearns helped me remember that men and women are on the same side—that someone was out there looking for me, and wanted me to find her. Since reading it, an amazing opportunity came my way, and I didn't blow it. Now we are dating seriously."

— Vincent R.

"Innately refreshing because it's honest; funny because it's true. Finally a guy comes clean."

— Gary H.

better love next time

better love

how the relationship that didn't last can lead you to the one that will

next time

J. M. Kearns

John Wiley & Sons Canada, Ltd.

National Library of Canada Cataloguing in Publication Data

Kearns, J. M. (J. Michael)
    Better love next time : how the relationship that didn't last can lead you to the one that will / J.M. Kearns.

ISBN 978-0-470-96488-0

    1. Man-woman relationships. 2. Separation (Psychology). 3. Mate selection. I. Title.

HQ801.K41 2011   646.7'7   C2010-906238-8

Production Credits
Cover design: Ian Koo
Interior design and typesetting: Adrian So
Cover illustrations: Jennifer Borton and iStockphoto/bortonia
Printer: Solisco Tri-Graphic Printing Ltd.

John Wiley & Sons Canada, Ltd.
6045 Freemont Blvd.
Mississauga, Ontario
L5R 4J3

Printed in Canada

1 2 3 4 5 TRI 15 14 13 12 11

To Debra

contents

introduction

Some relationships are casual or convenient, and when they end, it isn't too hard to shrug them off and move on. They don't linger in the psyche and they don't have much effect on the future.

And then there's true love gone wrong, the subject of this book. That hurts you big time upfront, but it also casts a negative spell that can mar your future relationships. Our goal will be to heal that hurt and break that spell.

Here is how the story goes. You fall deeply in love, and it is returned, and you invest yourself, heart and soul, in a life with someone, believing you have found the right partner. And then it all crumbles to the ground. When that kind of love goes wrong, it can be devastating. It feels as if a shadow has fallen across the world. As if judgment day came and you were found wanting, and now life as you knew it is over. It's a lonely, marooned feeling. Despair seeps through you. Your heart bends in pain; your ego protests.

And the last thing you want to do is to examine the failed relationship, and the damage it has done to you. You want to just toss it into the garbage. All that pain—and sadness, anger, guilt, sheer humiliation—makes you want to turn away and try to hide from it. Drown it, deny it. Try to pretend it didn't happen or it doesn't matter. Stomp it under your muddy boot, and trudge on under a dim sky.

So you do.

And then the months, or years, go by and you find yourself in a new relationship. And you notice little things happening, words and actions, that are strangely familiar.

You get together with a fabulous new leading man, but your previous relationship, neglected and dishonored, sits in the cheap seats revising the script—trying to make it the same as the old script. So you have to deal with it after all; but the new play is already in full swing and you need new lines to make the new love story work. You need a new character, a new self that won't take the fall like last time, won't be typecast in the same old role.

Where are you to find that new approach that will get better results?

The answer I'm about to give will be the same, no matter where you are in the story I just related:

- You may be still reeling from a breakup and nursing a broken heart.

- You may be farther down the road, but with less of the optimism you once had about romance.

- You may be even farther on: you've started something with a new partner, but in the back of your mind is a shadow, a fear that old patterns will repeat themselves.

Whichever situation you're in, the solution lies in what might seem like the most unlikely place: the past.

That is because failed relationships don't just hurt us; they also do *damage*. They impair our future ability to love and to live. And they consign us to a broken world, a world gone wrong, where our own best lights don't shine. They compromise our soul, making us think that we, and others, are unworthy. They program us for defeat.

You might think that if enough time has gone by, the past will have lost its potency. But scarily enough, that isn't true. As soon as you hit the road with a new relationship, look around and you'll find the past grinning at you from the back seat.

That's the fascinating thing. *Until dealt with, the past is always fresh.*

So what are we to do with this pesky past?

Well, it may seem trite, but the thing to do is face it down.

Like a monster in an old story, a failed relationship gets stronger and more terrible if you run from it, but if you turn and face it, it turns out to be not so scary, and pretty soon it wants to make peace with you. So the way to overcome it is to *face* it, sort it out, reverse the damage it did to you, shake off the bad lessons it tried to teach you and find the good ones it's holding back.

This may seem like a humble goal, to sort out the past. But in fact it can lead to seriously wonderful possibilities. When you heal the damage that was done to you, you regain the whole person you were meant to be, and you carry that person into your next relationship. And there's more. The relationship that didn't last holds glorious ore, in the form of lessons written in your own personal history, priceless lessons about how love should be and how it can work out right, when you attempt it again.

The adage says that those who don't understand history are condemned to repeat it. That is never more true than with love.[1]

---

1. The original saying was from George Santayana: *The Life of Reason* (1905): "Those who cannot remember the past are condemned to repeat it."

"Better luck next time," someone may say to a gambler who has lost; but it has a wistful sound—because pure chance doesn't offer much hope. My title tips its hat to that expression, but it embraces a different philosophy: finding better love *isn't* about blind luck; it's about learning from experience.

I hope this book will be good medicine for the troubles that ail you. I'll offer some laughter (because some of this stuff is too awful not to laugh at), and maybe some tears, and most of all I'll try to bring some understanding. There will be lots of stories, a mystery or two, and maybe even a murder along the way—failed love drives people to drastic places.

A side note: as we explore the interstices of the past relationship and the ways that it might try to sabotage you in the present, your mind may leap back, beyond your most recent love affair, to one that came earlier, which you sense is still affecting you adversely. That is all to the good: for many of us there is one formative romance that did the most damage, and that is the one most in need of illumination. So follow your nose to what seems relevant, and apply our process to it; you won't go wrong.

There are two aspects of achieving better love. One: processing the past. Two: getting past the past, finding your way with a new person, helped by the lessons you've learned. Sometimes you get to do one first, then face the other. Other times it all happens at once. You meet a new person and their merit leaves you no choice: you have to scramble and try to make this one work out differently.

Either way, it can be done. There is a way to listen to the past, a way to read failed relationships, that will clear the road to better love next time. I'm not saying your world will become predictable and under control, or that you can ever know exactly where things are going from day to day. Far from it. But you *can* get yourself on board a better world.

And in fact, isn't the worst thing about bad relationships their predictability? It can seem like you're caught in the endless loop of a bad romantic comedy. You *can* get out of that loop, but you can't do it by throwing away the movie. You need to face it. Watch it and understand it. Then it will carry you to the relationship you want. And even help guide you through it.

PART

I

REPAIRING THE EFFECTS OF THE BREAKUP

1

 the final slide to goodbye

_A_fter the iceberg hit the _Titanic,_ most passengers didn't know yet that the ship was going to sink. But there were ominous signs, and the feeling of festivity got just a little hollow. Odd things started happening, like distant screaming in hallways, an unseemly tipping of the floor, and oh, water underfoot. The musicians kept playing, and fine gentlemen and ladies lifted whisky glasses to their lips, but I'm guessing the single malt didn't taste quite right.

You lie in bed at night inventorying which household possessions are yours.

It's like that with a failing relationship. You go through months and months of feeling like maybe it's going to end, then it does and somehow it feels like a shock. Or it hits out of the blue—and then you notice all the clues that you missed. This last situation is worth pausing over: how can an intelligent person be unaware that their primary human is about to break up with them? Well, it could be that the partners are abysmally out of touch; then again it could be that they are blanketed in rituals, comfortable patterns that make them think they are still close, when all they have is the worn shawl of routine.

And there's another possibility: deception. A perfectly alert person can sometimes be fooled by a conniving lover. And that power of deceit is itself a sign, because people who are really in touch with each other can usually tell when the other person is hiding something.

Those doomed months are torture, however they shake out. So let's take a look around the listing vessel, and with a ghoulish giggle or two, note the awful clues that mark the final slide.

thirteen warning signs that a relationship is soon to end:

1. You feel like crying when the other person is nice to you.

2. The sound of him eating fills you with a homicidal rage.

3. You don't feel like yourself anymore, when he's around: your personality feels phony or distorted.

4. You find yourself being bluntly honest, objecting to his quirks that you used to put up with. (Could it be you have nothing left to lose?)

5. You have trouble planning anything for next year (or next month).

6. Your partner thinks he has told you things when he hasn't. (You're getting ready for dinner and he says, "That bonus check should be here by Thursday," and you say "What bonus check?" and he says, "I thought I told you about that . . ." This could mean you are no longer his primary ear.)

7.   Your social lives become completely separate.

8.   **You fight a lot more than usual; or worse than that, you stop fighting completely.** (It's an ominous silence when one person just lets thing slide, no longer wanting to engage with the other about the juicy issues that come up in your life together.)

9.   **To get away from your partner, you go to a favorite café. As you're settling down with your latte, you spot him in the corner, cradling his.**

10. **You are laughing with a good friend one day and you realize you haven't laughed like that for months or years.**

11. **It becomes painful for you and your partner to spend time with happy couples (or watch them on the screen).**

12. **You lie in bed at night inventorying which household possessions are yours.** (The food processor? Definitely.)

13. **You stop using your partner as a sounding board or a shoulder to cry on, because you assume he won't understand.**[1]

So many signs, signals, clues. Makes one wonder how anyone could ever be surprised by a breakup.

Interestingly, these warning signs don't necessarily indicate who is going to break off with whom. Signs 1 and 6 suggest that the "you"

---

1. There are a number of other signs that I didn't include here, clues that your partner is cheating. This is not a book about how to catch a cheater, but I will talk about the harm done by cheating and how to cope with it.

will be left by the other person. Signs 2, 4 and 10 suggest that "you" will do the leaving. Even with these cases, the more you think about them, the more uncertain they become. And with most of the others, you simply can't tell who is going to do the nasty deed.

So what determines who *does* pull the trigger? What provides the impetus to action? This question isn't as easy as it seems. Every answer just seems to spark a counter example:

- **The one who is suffering the most in the relationship breaks it off.** Response: but sometimes the other person feels so guilty that they call it quits. Or the reason one person is suffering is that the other person is getting ready to pull away.

- **The one who has grown tired of the other, or has fallen out of love, breaks it off.** Response: that isn't always true. The "unrequited" person, who is sick of loving and not being loved back, sick of under-appreciation, may very well have the strength to walk away.

- **The one who glimpses a better world, breaks it off to go there.**

Now we're getting somewhere. You are not likely to end a relationship unless you have a vision of the world you'll be in after the breakup, and you believe that *the new world will be better than the one you're in.*

But what if *both* people feel that way? Then who pulls the trigger?

That's easy. The one who is having a bad day.

This is our first glimpse of a fact I'll revisit later—one that carries many lessons and no small comfort.

Things are not as different between the (eventual) dumper and dumpee as one might expect.

It isn't that easy to tell them apart.

When a relationship is sick or dying, both people often know it, unconsciously or very consciously. So either one could decide to break it off; could declare that they've had enough.

Suppose it's you. For whatever reason, you find yourself ready to end it. That, unfortunately, does not mean the end of your problems. For you will now have to deal with a moral quagmire, that I call:

THE TANGLED ETHICS OF BREAKUPS

it's never the right moment to break up

It's an awful thing to say, but once you've decided to break up with your partner, the apparently minor issue of timing can become a huge obstacle. Something always seems to come up, just when you're finally ready to make your move.

> There is no moment when a fair-minded referee would say, "Okay, commit your foul now."

Let's face it, it's hard for most of us to play the bad guy; we would almost rather provoke the other person into doing the dirty deed. But if you have to be the perp, you don't want to compound the felony by hitting your partner when they're down.

Or when they're happy . . .

So your announcement gets postponed, sometimes for months or even years.

reasons why you can't break it off this week:

- His favorite aunt had a heart attack and is in the ICU.

- His high school reunion is coming around.

- Your best friends are celebrating their tenth anniversary.

- Thanksgiving is next week.

- Christmas is in two weeks.

- It's the Super Bowl.

- Valentine's Day.

- It's his birthday tomorrow.

- The family is gathering for Easter.

- He just got the big promotion he's been working towards.

- He had a really bad day; looks like he may be laid off.

- You had a really bad day and can't face any more stress.

- The coast is finally clear but things perversely improve between you.

Really, it's impossible to pick the right moment. There is no moment when a fair-minded referee would say, "Okay, commit your foul now." There isn't a morning when you wake up and your partner is standing there in a T-shirt that reads: *if you break up with me <u>right now</u>, it won't hurt me and won't cause any trouble.*

So what do many people do? They just pick any moment and strike. And that looks cold and cruel to the other person and to the world.

Or they wait till a fight erupts, till they're so mad at the other person that they don't give a damn. That would take care of it.

Or they nurse the impulse, lock it in some inner jewel box, bring it out when they're annoyed and finger it; it becomes a fantasy that gives relief during the bad times and is almost abandoned during the good times.

But not quite: there it remains in the box, creating a sort of permanent latent betrayal.

the family factor

When you're first getting to know a new person, there is (or should be) plenty of time to render a negative verdict without feeling too guilty. That's why I recommend that you exercise this privilege, look for compatibility, and walk away when you discover that it isn't there. Walk away early.

> "Dan, it's about pork chops with blueberries. I need them in my life."

Because it will be much harder, later. And one of the reasons for this is that your partner becomes family. After you've lived together for a while, after you've met and maybe bonded with each other's relatives, after you've gone through some ups and downs and weathered some rocky miles, you start to feel that you could no sooner abandon this person than your own parents or your own children. Maybe that basic loyalty is what keeps many couples together through the thin times. They just don't see it as an option to jettison the other person. So they make the best of things. In the old days, "till death do us part" had this meaning. You have now become my family, flesh of my flesh; you are now instated as part of my nature, closer than blood. Leaving you is unthinkable.

When the padlock of family snicks shut, it just seals in a larger ethical question that faces the would-be breaker-off-er. *How can you purposely do something that will make someone else less happy*? How can you administer a blow that will cause pain to someone you care about? This question is easier to deal with—or easier to avoid—if the relationship is causing you more discomfort and pain than him; because then you can just say, "A little pain on his side is okay if it relieves a lot of pain on mine."

When that won't work, a moral searchlight switches on . . .

sonya and the moral beacon

Sonya had lived with Dan for seven years. She made good money as a mortgage broker, and they lived in her house, on which she paid the note. Dan worked sporadically as a carpenter and seemed pretty content to eat the fine meals that Sonya cooked, to go out drinking with his buddies several nights a week, and to not worry very much about anything.

Although she was slim and brown-haired, she wasn't slim, brown-haired and bearded.

He was comfortable. She was restless. Nesting with Dan had felt good for a few years, but one day while she was cleaning up after dinner it dawned on her that she had become a mommy. That was what he needed, apparently. The fire in the bedroom that had once seemed to justify a lot of things, had now dwindled to an ember or two. So those other things loomed larger. Like, his idea of reading was the same biography of the same NASCAR driver, over and over again. Like, she couldn't tell him about her hassles at work, because he didn't have the patience to understand them. Like, she had met a banker. Oddly, his name was Dan too. Or Dan Two. He liked to be called Daniel.

Daniel wanted more of Sonya. Daniel had already cooked her a meal, one evening when they worked late at his place, and it was a good one, pork chops with blueberries, a cool Italian recipe that made Sonya think what it might be like to be with someone who shared her interest in cooking, not just her interest in eating. Daniel liked Sonya's stories about her difficult mortgage clients. Daniel liked details. Daniel also liked traveling, and hiking, and wine. So did Sonya.

But Sonya held Daniel off. She kept a distance from him, kept her heart unengaged. For example, she wouldn't let him kiss her— well, she did one time, when she ran into him at a café downtown and they sat on a couch in the corner. But it was too good. The kiss was way too good.

And that moral light was on. It shone on her, and it told her that loyalty is a virtue, that Dan was her family, that he would be devastated if she turned him out. He would be like a motherless child. Somehow, she didn't seem to have the justification to hurt an innocent human being.

She imagined what she would say to him. "Dan, it's about pork chops with blueberries. I need them in my life. You aren't providing them. So you have to go."

And she imagined Dan would say, "Hon, I can learn to cook pork chops. With . . . what?"

So she lingered in her limbo, a prisoner of her own conscience. And it might have gone on that way for years. But something saved her. She needed not to be in control, not to be responsible. And something took the control out of her hands.

Something called love.

One evening she sat at her job, in a state of extreme tension. She had had a fierce confrontation with a co-worker who was constantly trying to sabotage her. She had finally faced him and the battle had been nasty. And to her own surprise, she had won. She had exposed the guy's lying, made him back down; on top of that, her boss had monitored the scene from behind a cubicle wall, and had validated her afterwards.

So she had triumphed. The problem was, Sonya was still racked with adrenaline, and she needed someone to talk to, away from work. Dan wasn't even an option. So she reached out to Daniel. He was at home and she went there, and she told him everything and they laughed and they had a few drinks, and then they were making love with their clothes half on and there had never been any decision, it was already too far gone before her head even knew. Then they ate—he cooked for her again, *rigatone prima vera* this time—and then they got under the covers, and the next morning it rained, but it didn't matter, because Sonya, blessedly, was in love.

She had fallen. And when you fall, you aren't in control. You are a pawn of greater forces. It happens to you; you aren't making a choice. (Ask any romantic.)

And that has one great benefit. It turns the moral beacon off. What you can't help, you can't be held responsible for. Right?

So Dan was given his notice. Not easily, not without a lot of trouble; but it got done.

And things got off to a good start with Daniel. If Sonya had a physical type, Daniel was it. Unlike the short, stocky Dan, Daniel was tall, lean, bald, and had verdant chest hair. In this and many other ways, he was what Sonya was looking for.

So can we conclude that falling in love not only frees us from responsibility but invariably leads us to the right partner? Unfortunately, no. Because it turns out that Daniel had a physical type too, and Sonya wasn't it. Although she was slim and brown-haired, she wasn't slim, brown-haired and bearded. And just about the time that he and Sonya were talking about moving in together, Daniel met a nice doctor named Jim who was all three, and then Daniel did the unthinkable: *he* fell in love.

I would offer a couple of thoughts on this story. One is, it makes you wonder if it might not be better, when you are clearly with the wrong person, to face the moral music, leave that person, and take your knocks. In this case one suspects that Sonya was being played by Dan: he had a pretty good thing going and he knew how to keep it going. One also suspects that the price Dan would pay by being without Sonya wasn't so much higher than the price she was paying by being with him. Admittedly it's a hard line to draw; and you have to really ask yourself how unhappy you are before you go ahead and make someone else unhappy.

> There was a curious recovery in the desire department, now that Roxanne was a bit hostile.

The other "tangled ethics" take-away is that one begins to question the irresistibility of falling in love. It may seem like a force we can't contend with, an act of destiny that simply masters us, but there's something a little bit convenient about the way it popped up when Sonya needed it. I will return to the fascinating nature of what I call the In-love Reaction, in Chapters 16 and 17; for now let me say this: If it's right to leave somebody, then you don't need to fall in love in order to do it, and if it isn't right, falling in love won't justify it.

And now some more advice to the perp: if you're going to dump somebody, dump them and leave them alone.

the compassionate perpetrator

Bob the shipping clerk had a different approach. He met a lot of women at work, fellow employees and customers, so he had a lot of soil for his plow. His story: he was a serially monogamous guy. When he fell in love he was obsessive and ultra-romantic. He often chose women who at first resisted his advances. He got very wrapped up in each new one, absorbed in her to the exclusion of anyone else. But then, once she started to open her heart to him, something went wrong. The prospect of normalcy, of love being an everyday thing, made him feel a curious deadness within. He would feel his passion waning.

So it was time to move on, and Bob would unceremoniously break off with his gal, telling her that he was sorry, but he just didn't feel in love anymore. That's what he did with Roxanne, his latest conquest, who was a hair stylist of Asian extraction. Bob gently shared with Roxanne the regrettable news that the thrill was gone. He was sorry, but it couldn't be helped: these things are beyond our control.

The parting lasted a night or two. But then a different mood seized Bob, as it always did at this stage.

"She is lost, alone," he thought. "She may not be able to fend for herself. I had better check on her." So he called her. And sure enough, after a couple of hang-ups Roxanne was willing to talk to him, and it turned out that she was in an awful state: hurt, angry, lonely, in need of a shoulder to cry on.

"What shoulder better," Bob asked himself, "than mine?"

The fact that she was mad at him really bothered Bob. He didn't like anybody angry at him, ever. He hated to feel guilty, hated to be the bad guy. And the thought that she might speak to her friends about him (her friends whom he had caused her to neglect) was unbearable. He might be criticized or condemned. She might call him cruel, unfair, stupid, a loser. That wouldn't do. That had to be prevented.

On top of which, there was a curious recovery in the desire department. Now that Roxanne was a bit hostile, wary of him, she became quite appetizing again.

We're not trying for true love anymore, we have nothing to lose, and I feel like some pizza and TV.

"Do you want to go out for a coffee?" he asked her on the phone. She said yes, still shuddering from tears. They met and he was in love with the chance to comfort her, in love with her vulnerability. He told her she was a great person and a great catch, that she shouldn't take his rejection personally. He took her hand, gazed into her eyes. On the way back to her place, he put his arm around her. In the dorm he said, "Do you want to cuddle? Let's just hold each other." And it was sweet and hot like a good Chai latte.

Their "second" relationship lasted a while, not as long as the first one. And the next was shorter than that. Now they are "good friends" and Roxanne still hasn't gotten over Bob.

Out of this and similar stories comes . . .

a note to the perpetrator

- You can't be the bad guy and the good guy at the same time. So be the bad guy. Accept the role you've cast yourself in.

- Let the other person hate you and resent you. Let them call you every bad thing: mean, base, unloving, idiotic, a cad and a loser, a liar and a worm. They have a *right* to see you that way. You hurt them and disappointed them. You walked.

- Stay away. Even if you are tempted to give comfort, to defend your action, to assuage your own loneliness. To be "just friends".

- You will find that the playing field is somewhat leveled by what you've done. Knowledge is power, and now you've let the other person know the truth about your feelings, and about their prospects with you. Now they can see clearly—if you let them. The information you were withholding gave you an advantage; now you've lost it. That's the price you pay. Don't try to get it back.

- The person you've dumped will now have a chance to get over you and maybe find someone they'll be happier with. You may not like the sound of this; but it's your job to suck it up and let it be. *You can now be replaced;* in time you will be. This is another consequence of your action, so live with it.

- You have now become part of that person's past. You're going to fade into history. So fade.

On-again, off-again breakups. When these precepts are violated, as in the case of Compassionate Bob, what often happens is an on-again, off-again breakup. A couple, after all, have been each other's main companions, and they have more to offer each other than any third person can. And now that they've given up on winning it all, the stakes are lower, so it's not so scary. The worst has already happened . . .

It's tough being by yourself when you're used to someone else always being around. So when loneliness or boredom kicks in, one person or the other gets on the phone, and the backsliding begins. The feeling is: we're not trying for true love anymore, we have nothing to lose, and I feel like some pizza and TV. And I don't like eating pizza alone.

What really tangles things up is when you involve your friends in your breakup. In the case of Compassionate Bob, Roxanne had given a running report to her best confidante Jill, and even before Bob dumped her, the two women had agreed that things were not okay with him. He was a user and a narcissist; he didn't really care about Roxanne. Then he did break it off, and Jill supported Roxanne in the decision to be strong and deal with being dumped. By this time Jill had invested a lot of time and empathy into Roxanne's situation, and into the negative verdict on the relationship. Even Jill's husband Larry had gotten involved. All three agreed that things with Bob would never have been right, that Bob was bad news, that it was a mercy he had broken off with Roxanne, that now she could move on and find someone better.

Then Roxanne let Bob lure her back. Jill and Larry experienced this as a betrayal. They weren't able to do a 180 with all their beliefs and suddenly think bad Bob was a good guy. They felt as if Roxanne had been toying with them, manipulating them to take a position just so she could try it out. Were they supposed to be jerked around like puppets every time she changed her mind? They had helped her find the truth and now she was abandoning it. Eventually they were proven right, but their relationship with Roxanne was now added to the casualty total.

I hope that this little tour of the warning signs of a breakup, and the tangled ethics that a wannabe leaver has to pass through, may have put some perspective on your own experience, and helped cast it in less black-and-white terms. These matters are complicated on both sides, and the more you realize that, the more you can avoid reacting in a simplistic way. The discussion of the Perpetrator's Precepts and on-again, off-again breakups can alert you to how things may have been mishandled, and help you guard against ongoing mistakes.

Having pulled ourselves through the doorway of goodbye, it's time now to look at what lies outside it. It's time to take stock of the pain and hurt that lost love inflicts, and the injuries—material and spiritual—that result. A person in this situation is a little like a wounded soldier: in need of diagnosis, first aid, and a move to safety. Then their condition can be looked at more closely and injuries healed. That way they can live to fight a winning battle next time. (The enemy here is not your once or future partner, but the forces that wreck relationships.)

So we'll start by taking a hard, honest look at what a breakup often makes you feel. There are a bunch of reactions that it can cause, involving denial, hurt, despair, and anger. Sometimes several of them churn around inside you and take turns surfacing. We'll get to all of them, but we'll begin at the top of the list, with something called a broken heart.

2

 ## the sound of a broken heart

$\mathcal{T}$he heart is the engine of human life, the organ that says, "Yes, I'm going to keep on keeping on, keep on beating as long as I can." Its motto is, "Life is worth living, no matter how tough it gets." Never say die. We speak of someone "having heart" when they fight on through impossible conditions to reach a goal, especially when that goal involves someone else's welfare.

A broken heart is called that because it feels like a critical blow to this organ. We actually feel an aching in our chest and this last bastion of the will to live feels like it's been lanced. Sadness, pain, and loneliness well up from that fractured center and engulf us.

What event most typically causes all this? The loss of someone we love.

"Loss" meaning they are taken away from us. The simplest and most final way for this to happen is when death takes them. Someone loses a child, a parent, a spouse, or a best friend. They're gone from the earth and the survivor is left here without them; that can be a lot to bear. So we hear about one aging spouse who passes away, and not too long after, the other one dies of a broken heart. Tragic as it is, this outcome isn't hard to understand.

The one you've lost can still be seen, roaming the earth and maybe in the company of someone else.

And then there's a different kind of broken heart, where the person you lose goes right on living, and it is *their* choice that takes them away from you. That's the romantic variety, and to the pain of loss it adds the pain of rejection, and the madness-inducing feature that the one you've lost can still be seen, roaming the earth and maybe in the company of someone else. They're gone, and yet they're not gone.

This kind of broken heart is a little less straightforward. For it harbors a complication: *when you were left, the one you love got what they wanted.* But that doesn't mean it's less painful. A million sad love songs aren't wrong.

No, love is still love when its complaint is not against death, but against the very person who is the object of that love.

To understand that better, let's take a closer listen to this kind of plight. What does a broken heart say, in the tangled realm of romance?

The Words of a Broken Heart

I can't believe you've left me, you've spurned me
I can't live without you (I *won't* live without you . . .)
Please take me back
I love you so much, you *have* to love me
My heart is aching, I can't breathe, I can't walk, the sadness
is crushing me
I am so alone
Life can't be this cruel and unfair
See my misery and make things right
You are all that matters, you are beautiful, you are the one

I am nothing without you
Only you can make me happy

And the song goes on.

The pain of lost love is a terrible thing; it's devastating and it can have lasting consequences. But if you look at the lyric, is there a whole lot in it that concerns the well-being of the *other* person? Not really. It seems to be all about the "me", not the "you". The *you* may in fact be doing alright, may not be suffering much, but that isn't the *me's* concern here.

I walked the city and howled at the moon, and thought if only she could see my misery, she would take me back.

When you think about it, falling in love isn't all about the joy of giving. There's quite a bit of *getting* going on. Winning a great new partner carries a lot of benefits, many of them very satisfying to the receiver. Benefits like: the other person's attention, their admiration, the feeling of being important to someone, of being exciting, of being wanted sexually, the sense of being a scintillating member of society's crème. These are boons to the ego, every one, even though they're accompanied by a delight in giving to the other person. And there are other blessings that come with new love: the feeling of coming home, of being supported, the sense of having a plan, having a future, having hope; the sudden immunity from loneliness. It isn't surprising that losing all these things would crush one's spirit.

Unless one is the perp. The one who *chooses* to lose all these things. Then it might not hurt as much.

Now there's an odd turn of events. Why *would* someone choose to throw all this bounty away, breaking the other person's heart in the process? Let's ask the guy sitting a couple of stools down at the bar, the one who has a way of bringing things down to simple terms, like who gains and who loses. He has wavy blond hair, tired eyes, and a rumpled blue windbreaker. He's whiling away an hour with some peanuts and a beer; he doesn't act like he's paying attention but he is.

"Bar Guy, why would a person, let's say a dude, throw away all the advantages and pleasures of . . . "

"I heard you the first time," Bar Guy says. "Look at it this way. Maybe the dude wasn't *getting* all these goodies anymore. The heartbreaker no longer had so much to lose; in fact, he felt he had a raw deal, or not the deal he wanted."

That's a good point, friend. The guy was still the expediter of his lover's dreams, but his own dreams weren't coming true anymore.

When love is in balance, when it's win-win, all is well. There's a level playing field, power is evenly distributed, and both people feel like they are benefiting—like they are lucky to have the other. But that can change and things can get out of whack.

And here I have to say: Bar Guy, you didn't get it exactly right. What happens is not that the future heartbreaker (let's call him HB) isn't getting goodies anymore—not exactly. It's more that HB is starting to *withhold* goodies like admiration and attention, and that makes his partner (call her V) want them even more. Why is he withholding them? Because he has too much power in the relationship. V has slipped, either because HB seized too much power—he wanted it and he took it—or because his waning interest gave him an accidental advantage, not one he was purposely seeking. Or she slipped because she *gave* him too much power, by not standing up to him or, sadly, by admiring him too much.

"Yeah, but he still isn't getting the goodies he used to," Bar Guy says, cracking a peanut shell. "Now that she demoted herself, he doesn't *want* her admiration anymore."

Okay, that's true too. When a person stops valuing their partner as highly, they stop wanting that partner's gifts, and they start withholding their own, and that just makes the partner more desperate to get what used to be forthcoming. That creates neediness, which feeds on itself until the deprived partner starts to lose her self-sufficiency.

So HB begins to perceive V as a losing proposition.

So HB breaks up the relationship and V gets a broken heart.

Exactly this happened to me some years ago. I was the victim, I lost my footing and became needy and unsure, and I got my heart broken. I walked the city and howled at the moon, and thought if only she could see my misery, she would take me back. At one point I considered leaping out of the back seat of a moving car. I even started writing love songs.

I turned off the stage lights and left the theater.

And while I still thought I had a chance to get her back, my misery was unabated. It just wouldn't let go. I walked past her house, thinking she would see me in the night and relent. I called her. I showed up at places where I knew she went. I was the star of my own huge drama and I did get to be with her a few more times and came tantalizingly close to being restored. Or so it seemed: really I think she just didn't know what to do with me.

"Misery is a choice," Bar Guy says. "Look at the toddler who starts screaming when his mother comes into the room. He was fine a minute ago but now he needs to manipulate her. Or look at my ex-wife and me. We're all upset and can't even speak to each other—then the phone rings and we're normal with whoever is calling."

Sorry, I won't agree that I chose that misery, that heartache. But I will admit one thing. Once I accepted for sure that I could never win her back, my personal drama did ratchet down a few notches. When I could no longer imagine her as my audience, I turned off the stage lights and left the theater, went back to the everyday world.

I went back. But I wasn't the same. And it wasn't till years later that I realized what the true damage had been. My broken heart eventually passed, it got better. But I had other problems, and they were big. They were set to affect my attempts at romance for years to come. Later in Part One I will explore those kinds of longer-term problems, how to recognize them and vanquish them in order to get to a real love.

But first a practical question demands some answers. When you first find yourself with a broken heart, how do you deal with it?

My long-term answer will be found in Part Two of this book, on "Unlocking The Lessons of the Relationship." When you learn the lessons of a failed relationship, that helps you more than anything else to get over it and trade hurt for understanding. That is what will lead you towards a better relationship and thereby restore your optimism.

Which still leaves the immediate wall of pain that seems to be collapsing upon you. It's time for those first-aid measures I mentioned before.

3

coping with heartbreak

$\mathcal{S}$ome breakups are not forever, not even till next Tuesday. Some of them are just negotiating points, ways of dramatizing a fight, stations in the dance of courtship, temporary setbacks in the process of learning someone else and accepting the ways in which they change your world. Some breakups are just a way of generating a round of make-up sex.

If he hadn't done the deed, you might have been forced to do it down the line.

But in this chapter I am talking about breakups that feel more final, more definitive—and more tragic.[1] Where it looks like it's gonna stick. Situations where the person who ended it seems to have given the matter sober consideration and has declared in a measured way that it's over.

And where the result on the other person's side is serious pain.

---

1. In this chapter I'm also not talking about dissolutions of marriage involving children. In those cases it is usually best if the parties can maintain a civil or even friendly connection. What I am talking about is the stage of life where you are still trying to find your way to the major, lifelong relationship that you want, and you fall in love, and it goes bad and you get your heart broken. How do you pick yourself up, dust yourself off, and get ready to find a better love?

when somebody breaks your heart:

- Stay away from him. Don't reopen the wound. Don't invite him to be the good guy while also being the bad guy, as we discussed in Chapter 1. Don't turn for comfort to the person who broke up with you. Don't even turn to him for help, unless you absolutely have to.

- Meditate on the fact that this loss is primarily about you, not about him, as we saw in Chapter 2. Your pain isn't about your concern for him. Get perspective from that.

- If you are sad, enjoy the sadness. Realize that sadness is actually a valuable human state, a valid place. Read some sad poems, listen to some sad love songs. Own it, let yourself feel it, don't try to pretend you're not hurting.

- Find a friend you can talk to about it, someone you can be honest and vent with; or call a counseling line and talk to someone. Don't let this be a secret, private hole to crawl into.

- Again, don't go it alone. Once you feel a bit better, seek out good friends, make new ones if you have to, draw on whatever spiritual and emotional resources you have; get involved in the lives of others and do something for them. All this will shore up your self-esteem and put your own life in perspective.

- When somebody breaks up with you, it's actually their way of telling you that they're not the right person for you. The fact that they left you—they lost interest and didn't want to hang on to you—means they weren't for you. They have given you valuable information that could have taken years to discover. Don't shoot the messenger.

- If there was mistreatment involved, then you're definitely better off.

- If the relationship itself had become miserable, then the breakup is a mercy. There were probably advance signs that all was not well, as we saw in Chapter 1. So realize that if those clues existed, then this may not have been such a miscarriage of justice after all. If he hadn't done the deed, *you* might have been forced to do it down the line. Maybe you were already thinking of ending it . . . if so, don't worry too much that he beat you to the punch—the outcome would have been the same. Instead, be amused by the following lines, written by a talented poet I know. In it a woman imagines time stopping just before her boyfriend can break up with her.[2]

> If time stood still when you break my heart
> I could stop and think before you start
> I could laugh and say, "Now I've got to go,
> This love of yours makes me sink too low."
>
> If time stood still, I could dance around,
> Kick some dirt and do the town,
> And then I'd see on the way back home
> That it's time for you to be left alone.[3]

---

2. Of course the words of the poem could equally well be spoken by a man; but for convenience I'll follow its feminine point of view.

3. Part of a poem by R. Parigini, used with permission.

And now if you'll indulge me in an English 101 moment, we'll get a payoff that helps lift the ignominy of being the one who was left. The speaker in this poem is saying, in a wonderfully vivid way, that she who is about to be left has just as much right to break it off as her jilting partner has. He just gets there first; he's quicker on the draw. But if time were to stop at the split second before he rejects her, and she knew what was coming, she would be able to clearly see that he is bad news in her life, that he brings her down, and that she should leave him.

If time stood still—for him. The speaker gleefully imagines that her boyfriend is frozen in time—parked in place—while she is launched into a happy celebration of her emancipation from the one who has in fact kept *her* from being free. She dances, does the town, kicks up her heels and rollicks. Then, on her way back to the place they share, she sees clearly that the *boyfriend* is the one who needs to be left.

So realize that his leaving you was just a quirk of time, a trick of sequence designed to make you feel like the victim. But really it could have been the other way.

- You may feel anger, a desire for revenge, a desire not to let the other person get away with it. That's not your heart, that's your ego talking, and we'll deal with it a little later. For now, resist the temptation to let him know how you're feeling and what he has done. If that's a demand for justice, it's misplaced. The problem is, you won't get justice from him, and you *will* keep the wound open and maybe cause more strife.

- Use your love for the person as a way of accepting what has happened. Remind yourself that if you really love him, then you want him to get what *he* wants. Use the unselfish part of your feelings as a balm for the other part.

- Don't force the other person to tell you why. You can figure it out for yourself (we'll discuss how later), and your own answers will help you more.

- Don't threaten the other person.

- Make a clean break. Get gone. He will have to deal with a world that doesn't have you in it, that he is responsible for. And (if this matters) that is the only way he will ever "get" the enormity of what he has done. Then he may come crawling back. Even if you are tempted to reconcile—*especially* if you are tempted—don't make it easy.

- Don't pick up the phone when he calls. Don't do it. The time to talk was before he broke up. If he had asked to talk about things back then, without threatening to leave, that would have been fine.

- If he makes a concerted appeal to come back to you, don't say yes unless:

  · he explains why he left, in a way that you believe, and then explains why those reasons don't apply anymore,

  · you've thought over the whole thing and learned the lessons of the relationship as I'll discuss later, and you still think he's the right guy and you want to pursue it, and

  · he wants to come *all the way* back. (If he wants to be just friends, wish him well and show him the door. Tell him you'll consider his idea in a year and then *close* the door behind him.)

special pleadings: when false information was involved

There is an exception to the foregoing advice about making a clean break.

That is when you feel that part of the reason for your broken heart—part of what hurts so bad—is that the breakup was avoidable. It should never have happened because *it was based on false information.* You could deal with the breakup if it had been on valid grounds, but you can't deal with losing this person because of a mistake. So you want at least to set the record straight, before you retreat into silence. And you hope (even if you don't admit it) that just maybe, this correction might heal the rift and bring your lover back.

> You can't deal with losing this person because of a mistake.

And I say, go for it. Communicate the relevant information to your other half.

However, there's a danger that this exception could, if interpreted too loosely, become the crack through which all the earlier good advice drains away. So I want to make it clear before going on, what I'm *not* saying here.

I am not saying:

- that if you disagree with the breakup and think it is a mistake, you should contact your ex and argue about it. *Most* people who are on the receiving end of a breakup disagree with it!

- that if you feel bad about things you did that may have pushed your partner away, you should bombard him with apologies.

- that if you feel what happened wasn't deserved, you should plead that case. Again, most broken-hearted people feel that way.

What I *am* saying is that if you honestly think that either you or someone else conveyed false information to your partner that caused him to break off the relationship, there is no reason why you shouldn't let him know the truth.

Here's a familiar story. Liz and Fitzwilliam were dating, and though things were stormy between them, there was a very strong connection, sexually, intellectually, and on many other levels. It looked as though they would find their way through the rapids and reach the smooth waters. But evil George had a fancy for Liz, whose character and beauty would be nice adornments to his life, and he had a history with Fitzwilliam that he was able to distort into nasty lies. So George told Liz how mean, arrogant, and ungenerous William had been to him, and Liz spurned Fitzie's offer of marriage, leaving him with a broken heart.

What should Fitzwilliam do in this situation? Exactly what he does: he sends a letter to Liz, informing her in detail what *really* happened between himself and George; a sad tale that reveals that George, not Fitzwilliam, is the snake in the grass. Liz has a lot of trouble accepting this, but it begins a process that ends with the right lovers being happily united.

So this is my advice, when the breakup was caused by the conveying of false information. (It applies whether you were the source, and miscommunicated or were misinterpreted by your lover; or a third party was the source, as in our story.[4] The right thing to do is correct the information, without asking your lover to return.

---

4. Which is of course Ms. Austen's story, *Pride and Prejudice*, recklessly simplified.

Convey the true facts to your ex, but don't pressure him to take you back.

E-mails are a little too casual, too easily ignored, and too easily forwarded to others.

That might best be done by snail-mail, not in an e-mail. It may sound quaint in the Internet age, but e-mails are a little too casual, too easily ignored, too easily forwarded to others, and too apt to be dashed off in a reckless way. Try an old-fashioned letter, and make it calm, objective, and fair-minded. Don't ask for anything. Just give the needed information.

Another scenario is worth looking at, which illustrates why in most cases it's not a good idea to try to win back the one who broke your heart.

frank's overkill

When Frank broke off with Nina, she knew he "didn't really mean it." He had overreacted. So she was inclined to cajole him back into her life.

They had had a spat, and when she thought about it, Nina realized she had started it. But that didn't mean Frank hadn't made the crucial contribution.

She had given him a hard time because he was trying to study for his accountant exam on a Friday night. She had guilt-tripped him about not taking her out for dinner, and so he gave in, but then dinner was a disaster (bad mussels, followed by a night of retching) and Frank didn't get his act together that weekend and flunked his exam the next Monday, not for the first time.

So Frank got really mad, which was the only kind of mad he seemed to be *able* to get. That was Frank's problem. Moderate anger wasn't his forte. He had grown up in a household where such emotions were suppressed, and was uncomfortable with them. The result was he bottled them up until they exploded, at an intensity out of all proportion to the provocation. On this occasion, as usual, he had gone ballistic. He said that Nina was selfish and shallow and mean. He said she was a threat to his serious goals; that with her around he would never make his way. He said he couldn't feel good about his future unless they stopped seeing each other. Then that thought seemed to feed on itself and it escalated into goodbye.

"Why didn't you just say no to dinner?" Nina asked.

"Because you're hard to say no to. I would have been too distracted to study."

Then a week went by and Nina thought it over. What broke her heart was the sense that this hadn't been the "real Frank." It seemed too sad that they should not see each other anymore only because his anger had made him say things *he didn't really mean.* She knew he had a break-it-off reflex to get him out of the woods when he needed to express annoyance. An irrational outburst shouldn't be allowed to kill a valuable relationship.

> "Why didn't you just say no to dinner?" Nina asked.

Did that mean that she should wheedle and plead him back into her life?

Not at all.

They hadn't even reached the "living together" stage. If they got more serious, this pattern would only recur, because Frank hadn't faced his issues and Nina wasn't going to be his doormat. The best thing Nina could do was accept the breakup. If at some point Frank saw the light and crawled back to her, asking for another chance, she shouldn't even listen to that, unless it was accompanied by some proof that he was going to get help and do better. Which he never would, if she did the work for him.

Summing up this section: a broken heart needs to be handled with care by its owner. It needs time on its own, support, and a chance to recoup.

And that's only a piece of the story. We have talked about the more obvious effects of a breakup and how to deal with them, but we are only part way to the truth. There are more covert influences at work. In order to stop them from sabotaging the future—in order to get to the place where it's possible to enter fully into a new relationship—we need to drill down to a deeper layer.

By way of doing that, I am going to present a mystery story. It will be a classic case of romance on the rocks—love gone wrong. Our job will be to figure out who the culprit is. Who caused the mayhem, and profited from it? The answer may be surprising . . .

4

heather's train ride to hell

a mystery

*I*t should have been the start of a fun weekend for Heather.

She was on a train packed with rowdy college students, all traveling to another city to watch their team play in a crucial football game.

Justin, the guy she'd fallen in love with six months earlier, was with her, and so were their best friends, Megan and Tim. Megan and Tim weren't a couple, but that almost made it better: they were more available. They all had taken a rental house a month earlier, and it seemed to be working out.

Heather had never quite shed the childhood mockery of carrot hair and pasty white skin.

The train was packed with undergrads, but even high-toned grad students like our four had gotten caught up in the team's exploits this year. After years in the cellar, this team had a chance to win it all.

On the train, Heather and her three friends grabbed two seats that faced each other, formed their own enclave, and started drinking. They were all in the psychology PhD program. Justin was the most brilliant, already renowned on campus, a guy from a working-class family whose keen intellect had won him full scholarships all the way up, and who was revered for his ability to challenge eminent professors and rattle them. He was also a barrel-chested dude with long, wavy hair, fiery blue eyes, and a strange dent in his high forehead that made him look pirate-like. He was one of those men who put the lie to the notion that academics are somehow less manly than the rest of the male population.

Heather had been surprised when Justin made a play for her last July. Her surprise hadn't stopped her from a total, abject, trepidatious surrender of her heart—the first of her life. She was an auburn-haired beauty, but she didn't know it: she had never quite shed the childhood mockery of carrot hair and pasty white skin. Intellectually, however, she was just as aggressive as Justin—maybe more so. Since grade school Heather had been really good at debating. She wasn't that smart about people's emotions, but she had a remorseless head for logic and could detect a contradiction at thirty yards. Her best essays were the ones where she picked holes in someone else's theory. If Heather had a problem, it was that she lived too *much* in her razor-sharp mind. Her childhood peer group had made fun of that, too.

Then there were the two friends. Tim was a former English major who liked Jung. He had an open face and was a great guy to talk to. That left Megan. Megan was a former tomboy who had blossomed into a curvy colleen with chestnut hair. She was good at sports, very comfortable in her own body, aware of her allure and playful in her use of it. She never really stopped flirting, with men or women, and was the sparkplug of any party.

But what started happening on the train, almost immediately, was that Justin and Megan went all intellectual. Instead of light talk about football, Justin launched into an intense discussion of his latest idea for his thesis (he had come up with a new kind of personality test). Megan seemed to drop her femme fatale thing; she pulled out a pad of paper, donned her glasses which somehow made her look even cuter, and started making notes. Justin was sitting beside Heather, but she felt like a pallid moon. It seemed to her that Justin and Megan were like two prospectors standing in a rapid stream, too enthralled by the gold in their pan to notice the coming night.

Heather was very aware of Megan's easy beauty, of her unforced femininity. She felt freakish by contrast, like a bony albino with nothing to say. The two were getting creative, spawning theory like overactive salmon, and Heather suddenly twigged that she herself wasn't good at inventing new things. How had she missed that?

Then an awful thing happened. Megan reached over and touched Justin's knee, and said, "You know? I've always thought the problem with personality tests is that they assume the person you are now is who you are *meant* to be."

Justin stopped. Stopped moving, stopped breathing. Then he grabbed her hand.

"What? What?" Megan said, her eyes as serious as Heather had ever seen them.

Finally he spoke. "Most of us are damaged," he said. "We should be trying to test for who we were *before* we were damaged. That is the 'type' we should be guided by."

Heather and Tim gave each other a wry look, as from one person who doesn't exist to another.

That was the beginning. An hour later Heather came back from the trashed bathroom in the rear car to find Justin sitting next to Megan, papers spread out on their thighs, a laptop going, and their heads pressed together as they perused the screen for more gold. *I've never had any claim on him,* she thought.

Then Heather, who wasn't used to drinking, nodded off, but in a dream she seemed to hear Justin say, "We have to do this together. We'll make history."

That night they all crashed in a common room on the enemy campus, and there was no way to escape the blossoming of the new romance. Megan and Justin had always had a teasing, playful rapport, but now, infuriatingly, they were strangely respectful and almost shy. Between discussions of their revolutionary personality theory, they were asking each other solemn questions about their childhoods, and they kept finding miraculous correspondences.

And they were eying each other in an increasingly physical way.

Heather had no place else to be, had nothing to do but witness. For a while she tried to act as if things were normal, but she had begun to plummet on the train and the scene in the common room accelerated her fall. Though tenor-voiced Tim tried to distract her and keep things light, inside she was engaged in a terrible bout of destruction. Her whole self-worth was being dismantled, in a way that made it seem as if it had never existed. She was already clear that she was physically unattractive, had nothing to say, and was not meant to be an academic. Other people were capable of formulating new ideas; that was what you were there for; and she had nothing. Her PhD aspiration was a fraud.

A corrupt counselor had for a long time been whispering in her ear.

The last nail in the coffin came Monday when the four were back in their house and Justin and Heather slept together again. Heather had never really been confident in bed, not like Justin was: she had never quite felt a match for his buccaneering zeal, either as a physical specimen or as a sexual performer. Now she felt so plain and lifeless that he soon sensed her non-involvement, detoured into a wooden cuddle, and went to sleep.

She lay there thinking there was no real reason for her to take up any further space in this world. She went for a walk in the ochre night and found no evidence to the contrary. She was hurting too bad to cry. With a dead pain in her throat, she felt she wasn't *worth* crying over. When she got back to the house, Megan's door was closed, and Justin was gone from their bed.

Heather stayed in the house for another two months, which was a mistake. Megan and Justin made a ludicrous attempt to hide their new status that only rubbed it in.

the villain unmasked

And now, my detectives, we must ask: who was the culprit in this calamity?

The answer was pretty obvious to Tim. He said, "I can't believe what Megan did to you." Heather tried that theory on for size, and at times she believed it, and at times she blamed Justin for lack of loyalty; but something about the moment on the train when the two of them had hit it off, chilled these hot accusations and gave Heather a sadder, sicker feeling. Something else was to blame . . .

In spite of his condemnations, Tim stayed on in the house.

Not so Heather. She dropped out of the graduate program and moved into a room far from campus. She wasn't really okay for years.

She wasn't okay until she figured out what had really happened to her.

It wasn't a broken heart, as she had initially (and for a long time) thought. Or at least that wasn't the most important thing.

By the time Heather figured it out, she was a social worker, and a damn good one, and she had revealed a surprising knack for seeing into people. She was also starting to be interested again in romance; and although she didn't know it, she was on the verge of a better relationship.

What had Heather figured out? Only this: Rather than a broken heart, the crux of the Justin disaster was that her pride got demolished. Or rather, her already shaky sense of self-worth was test-ed too harshly and exposed.

In order to sort all this out, Heather had to delve into her own psyche and admit that before she even met Justin, she had real problems. She was overdeveloped in the smarts department and underdeveloped emotionally. She was insecure about her own sexuality and about her own physical appearance. She was also insecure about her intellect. She had always gotten by on razor-sharp logic and was in fact a smart aleck, covering up her fear of inadequacy under a veneer of cool aggression. Deep down she had been terrified that she had no original thoughts, that she was just a critic. That terror, she now realized, had been the main thing standing in the way of her forming new ideas. And maybe all of that had clinched Justin's allure: he had the very strengths she lacked, so by association with him she could "borrow" them.

But what she had done was bite off more than she could chew. She was a growing thing, still in need of development and nurturing. She needed a chance to find her own potential, discover value in her-self, and work on it. Justin was too much, too soon.

the corrupt counselor

But as Heather thought it through, she saw that an unwholesome presence—a corrupt counselor—had for a long time been whisper-ing in her ear. She pictured it as a yellow toad that had emerged from her ear, perched on her shoulder, and told her things. The toad had told her not to risk anything that might expose the awful truth about herself. It told her to disguise her shaky self-image from herself and others, and to prop it up by nearness to Justin. But it couldn't protect her from reality. Its choice of Justin as a lover just precipitated the moment of truth.

When Heather saw all this, she saw that although she had "fall-en in love," hard, with Justin, she had never really loved him. She couldn't. Her interfering adviser was too nervous to let her. She then saw that the loss of Justin to Megan was not the loss of love, but rather a scary opening of a vista on her own truth.

She saw that maybe her history could have been different. If the toad had been quiet and she had gone more bravely on her own path, and perhaps had been with a man equally unformed and uncertain, that moment of insight might never have crashed upon her in such a violent way. Maybe there could have been a steady growth. But it had happened the way it did, and she had listened to the voice and obeyed it and got hurt. Fortunately when she figured it all out, it was by no means too late for her to recover the Heather she wanted to be.

So we have our culprit. It wasn't Justin, or Megan, or even Heather. It was the toad. The Soul River Saboteur.

The voice that whispers to us about our dignity and our status. The Promoter of Pride.

The human ego.

Now that we've caught the criminal, I propose to incarcerate him for awhile. We'll keep him behind bars and examine him, and we'll look into what other nefarious things he's been up to. Just how wide is this scoundrel's path of destruction?

And how do we deal with the damage he does to love?

5

the ego's twisted agenda

*W*e've got the toad in stir. That nosy chaperone, that overzealous coach who inflicts his bad judgment on us—I'm calling him the ego. Am I on solid ground in doing so?

We talk about people's egos all the time. We say so-and-so has an inflated ego, and so he behaves badly. Someone else is lacking in the ego department. We may even have a dim sense that Freud said something on the topic. What is this mysterious part of the human being called the ego? And how does our romantic success depend on it?

Sigmund Freud, the black-bearded Viennese man who invented psychoanalysis, thought of the human psyche as a sort of unruly conversation among three characters: the ego, the superego, and the id.[1] His id was a gargoyle churning with primitive impulses; his super-ego a stern moralist planted by our parents. That left the ego, which he

---

1. Freud (1856-1939) used German words meaning the "I", the "over-I", and the "it" for these entities. His English translator chose to use the Latin terms we're familiar with—ego, super-ego, and id—which seem to have a dark power of their own. Freud was a trenchant observer of the human psyche, and shakier theorist, who gave the world the insightful theory that neurotic patterns are not just odd behaviors needing to be somehow eradicated, but have a purpose and meaning that therapists need to decode.

saw as the everyday self that tries to survive in the face of constant harassment by the other two inmates.

But out here in the world of non-psychiatrists, the word *ego* followed its own current to a different place. It ended up meaning something akin to pride or conceit, something toxic. That's how I'm using it—only more so. I'm sticking that label on the saboteur that Heather identified in her life: a stowaway, an interloper, a scheming toad who whispers insidious advice to the unwary self.

(It's also possible to use the word "ego" in a positive way, as in "I wish I had a strong ego like you". But I will call that positive quality "self-worth", and for clarity, will confine the "ego" label to the negative part of the psyche that I have pinpointed.)

We want to understand how the ego interferes with romantic relationships, so we can free ourselves from its influence. In order to do that, we need a more general picture of how it operates.

So with the toad safely in jail, I sent a team of investigators to follow his tracks backwards to a stagnant pond near the railroad tracks. There they found an old storage shed, littered with broken hearts and failed dreams. In a dark corner they discovered a driftwood plaque. A flashlight revealed its title: **The Sacred Wisdom of the Ego**. They read on:

1. I am the best—it's a foregone conclusion.
2. The worst thing is being mocked or demeaned by others.
3. The second-worst thing is not to get enough credit, not to be recognized and praised when you achieve great things.
4. It's more important what other people think of you than what's true.
5. Don't take risks, because failure hurts too much.
6. It's better not to find out about any areas you are weak in. To be tested, or helped, is to be insulted.

7. It's not how you play the game, it's whether you win or lose.
8. Make war, not love (provided you have the advantage).
9. Humility is for sissies.
10. It's all about me.

From this document a lot was learned about the ego's basic motivations. Its agenda is to inflate and protect its owner's status/ranking at all costs. Unfortunately this tends to interfere with the very things that could actually *earn* the status that the ego craves. And that's how the victim is cheated.

Photos, memos, and old newspapers stained with pond scum were also found in the storage locker. These creepy souvenirs led our team to other revealing stories:

- One of the ego's victims was called Joe. Joe was hired by a software company. For several days, he and three other new recruits gathered around their supervisor Alan, who sat at a computer demonstrating various routines, like how to look up a customer record, check it against various databases, and then correct it. Every now and then Alan would say, "Okay, who wants to drive?" and one of the new recruits would sit down and try to duplicate the moves they had just observed.

  Brenda did pretty well; she had a very good rote memory. Sean immediately got lost and had to be talked through every keystroke. Jessica was very confident and tried to do things her own way, getting into big debates with her teacher. All of them gradually learned. Except Joe. Joe's ego told him, "Never forget, you're the best. So you can't risk looking stupid in front of other people. Stay back, don't volunteer."

  A healthy person wants to know what he is doing wrong, wants to wade in and make mistakes so he can improve. Joe's dignity couldn't allow that. On day four Alan forced him to sit at the computer and he was so far behind that he got humiliated.

- Wendy was a country singer who had enormous natural talent, a strong voice and an unaffected delivery that could make a good song great. Not to mention fine-boned beauty. Her first single went to number one and she was soon at the top of the business.

  Unfortunately her ego, which till then had stayed out of the way, now stalked onto center stage. And like a good ego it was obsessed with protecting this fabulous new feeling of being exalted. This meant getting rid of anyone who still saw her as a mortal who might need advice or guidance. Soon the people who had steered her to success were gone, replaced by sycophants.

  Wendy's songs fell off the charts and she ended up doing very dubious things on reality TV.

  Wendy's sense of her own importance became so huge that she saw herself as a messiah sent to save ordinary people. She would weep with false humility at the height of a concert, when she was really feeling transported by her own divine wonderfulness. Her songs—now all chosen by her—became pretentious and phony. A good song would have been wasted anyway, because her performances only had one message: "how great I am."

  For some reason, Wendy's songs fell off the charts and she ended up doing very dubious things on reality TV.

Yes, the conniving ego gets in the way of a lot of the things that a healthy person might want: for example, to choose the right thing, to learn and grow, to do good work.

I gaze appraisingly at my laptop where I just entered these words. I'm about to type "And to love" when the commuter train I'm on heads into a tunnel, distracting me.

A healthy ego, like great acting, disappears.

But the man sitting next to me on the train has been looking over my shoulder. With a bird-like face, he's thirty-something, short-haired, and has a not-quite-put-together look that says corporate casual. He closes his *Reckless Guide to Oracle* and says, "Hey! That was good what you said about Joe the trainee. He won't learn if he doesn't try. But you've got it all wrong about ego."

"I do?"

"Yeah," says Corporate Guy. "You're not going to get anywhere in the business world if you don't have confidence, which by the way is based on self-esteem."

"Confidence," I say. "That certainly is something we all need. When you face a challenge, it helps to believe that you are good at this, and if it's a *really tough* challenge, it helps to know you are *really good*. But that's not the same as ego. Confidence is based on reality; it's usually earned through effort, discipline, dedication. The desire to excel at something can be a healthy thing."

"So what's ego based on?"

"Smoke and mirrors. The ego wants so badly to believe you're the best, that it treats conflicting evidence as a nuisance. Truly confident people usually have their egos under control."

"And be careful with self-esteem—it's a slippery slope," says the passenger on my other side (it's a crowded train). She has frizzy brown hair and shrewd eyes. Her briefcase has a Dept. of Education insignia on it. "It's an overrated concept," she adds. "It really messed up our schools."

"Kids have to be given self-esteem," Corporate Guy says.

"That's what we thought," she answers. "There was no such thing as too much of it, and you mustn't do anything to damage it. Self-esteem was like sacred ground. The only thing is, that meant you had to lie to kids. You couldn't give them a failing mark. So you end up shielding them from reality. You end up with a bunch of graduates who think they're terrific and don't have basic skills."

"And now their egos have sprouted like ghastly tubers," I say. "Taking over the garden."

The bottom line here is that the best ego is an ego that is asleep, invisible, forgotten. A healthy ego, like great acting, disappears. **People's best moments are in an ego-free zone.**

Now that we've seen our prisoner's *general* M.O., we can better understand his fine contributions in our area of interest—romance. Our defendant cuts a wide swath through human life, but his greatest crimes may be his crimes against love. It is the best thing he undermines, and he may well be its worst enemy. By exposing him, we can rescue love from his clutches.

Loving someone involves vulnerability and effacement of the self. It also risks rejection and heartbreak. To the yellow toad, these are outrages. His designs against them—and our countermeasures—will be the subject of the next chapter.

6

the romantic ego

dangerous when wounded

$\mathcal{I}$n the case of Heather, two chapters ago, we saw one way that the ego can stop a person from loving. Heather had a hungry ego that wanted her to be a hot shot in academic psychology and in romance, so it had taken the liberty of ordaining that she already was. Never mind the minor detail that she had yet to develop in these areas. Never mind that behind the false front of a sarcastic personality, she was afraid to leave her logical comfort zone and try to be creative, and she was emotionally immature. Her ego, being personally responsible for these failings, did not want them revealed.

That meant that Justin, her sensational new beau, was a serious problem; because his very nature was designed to expose Heather's problems. He was, to be blunt, out of her league. He was much more accomplished than she—and was good at detecting inadequacies in others. So Heather's ego watched him with a wary (and covetous) eye, alert to the danger he represented. He could ruin all its hard-won illusions, could burst its flimsy bubble.

Fear is like a straitjacket that pinches the heart. Heather couldn't love Justin, because deep inside she was afraid of what he might make her realize. He was a painful epiphany waiting to happen. So she played it careful, sucked up to him and borrowed his sheen, as long as she could . . . and then they got on that train.

If we look at the Justin side of the equation, we will see another thing the ego prefers over love.

> **He was frequently in awe of her, and she of him, just enough to keep them both honest.**

Justin was a very talented man, and had already written some distinguished psychology papers. But he also had a vigilant ego. And it saw in Heather a person who could be of service. She didn't think of Justin as a mere mortal like herself. And when he fell for her, he fell for that. Her adoration fit very well with his sense that he was, after all, a superior being. Heather's insecurity and inferiority were the perfect buttresses to sustain his self-worship. If he had been a better (stronger) person, Justin could have seen through her weaknesses to the talent underneath, could have treated her as an equal and nurtured her. But her fear was his invitation to arrogance, and her reticence was his spotlight.

Justin was capable of better things. When he hooked up with Megan, her greater confidence and prowess (than Heather's) trimmed his ego's sail. He was frequently in awe of her, and she of him, just enough to keep them both honest. They made a good team. They came to love each other and they lasted.

So those are two of the ways the ego can sabotage love: by raising one's partner into a threat, or by lowering one's partner into a reflection of one's own glory. And there are other, more everyday, ways.

- *Zero-sum games.* Have you ever been in a relationship where you felt constantly worried that you would lose and the other person would win? Some people bring this out in each other, and every facet of daily life can become a form of combat. The dishes need doing and neither person wants to lose the battle known as "It's your turn." Conversations morph into put-down sessions. You can't share feelings because the other person will see them as a sign of weakness. You feel as if you are constantly under attack. Every gain by one person is seen as a loss for the other, so you can't even share moments of success. Hearts are banished from the scene, and we are left with two egos fencing in a lonely space.

- *Play.* One of the things people do when their egos are asleep, is they *play.* Playing usually involves taking risks, though it may not seem that way when it's happening. For example, when two people concoct a comedy routine to portray a friend who annoys them, that involves risk. It's improv, and it requires trying things that may fall flat. You have to be comfortable enough with the other person not to worry that they'll judge you. If one person is afraid of coming off as less than brilliant, his humor will be brittle and he may infect the other person with his fear. When you see a relationship where the partners don't seem to be able to reach a place of pure play, look for the egos that are taking the air out of the room.

So the toad turns out to have quite a rap sheet. We've exposed his crimes against ongoing relationships; now it's time to get back to breakups and their aftermath. You might think a breakup would strip the ego of its power, but quite the opposite is true.

the mafia don

As far as the ego is concerned, nothing is more dangerous than risking your heart out there in the big, bad world. That's because losing at love, in the ego's view, is a reflection on our whole worth as a human being—not just on our performance in that one area. Our love score becomes our life score.

That makes sense, if you consider that mating may be the highest stakes game that we humans play. When you attach yourself to one partner and form a couple, all nature vibrates with the exciting Darwinian news that these two people are going to try for the brass ring—the chance to reproduce and thereby defeat death. It's a risky, scary enterprise, not one to be attempted with just anyone. It's your genes betting that his genes are the right ones to fuse with. It's an act of supreme trust, faith, and courage. It's a man in a casino saying, "I am *not* a gambler, I know the odds and I'll stake my reputation on this number."

When you pick someone to love, in front of the world you are saying, "You shall know me by this choice. This is me, this is who I am."

Small wonder that the ego watches all this with great concern. This is a huge opportunity for humiliation. In fact the ego advised against the whole thing, had to be excluded from the final conference where the heart's decision was made. The ego already feels maligned by that slight.

Our love score becomes our life score.

And then, months or years later, you get dumped or spurned or replaced. Your broken heart lies in the public square and that means your whole worth has been trashed, your dearest gamble repudiated. Your leap of faith, your attempt to sing your own beautiful song for all to hear, has met with scorn.

Like a mafia don, the ego values respect above all else. An insult cannot be left unanswered: that would be bad for business. In extreme cases, this means retaliation. There are two ways it can go:

1. The ego says: I buy that you don't want me anymore.[1] But not wanting me is not acceptable behavior. So something must be done to punish you. Revenge must be had.

2. The ego says: I *don't* buy your story. Not wanting me is not *possible*. You are mistaken about your own feelings and you need to be corrected. Therefore I will take control of your life and make it right again for both of us.

In Case 1 we get a scorned lover throwing her beloved's undergarments onto the street and posting his worst photos on Facebook, or in harder cases, angry spouses jeopardizing themselves and their children for the sake of a vengeful divorce settlement.

Case 1 can easily shade into Case 2, where the spurned lover simply rejects the premise. A cool way to accomplish this is to carry on as if nothing had happened. Continue to call the ex and talk love-talk on the phone, send amorous gifts, show up by surprise at the ex's house (or in their bed). The next, more severe step would be to get the rival out of the picture, not so much for the sake of punishment as for control. The goal is to rid the loved one of the distraction that has been leading them astray. This might take the form of filling up the rival's voicemail, adding salt to their gas tank, or implicating them in a recent spate of bank robberies.

Although I would hope you and I won't encounter it in real life, there's a more dire example that I want to mention—the movie *Fatal Attraction*. We've all watched the story and been chilled by it, but what bears remarking is how nakedly it displays the ego's way of thinking. An assault on the offending reality—that's what

---

1. The ego should say, "You don't want *my owner* anymore." But the ego confuses itself with the human it belongs to, and claims to speak for him.

it so well captures. The Glenn Close character simply wants to dismantle the happy home that contradicts her theory of things. She is like an advocate run amok; her single-minded premise is that the Michael Douglas character loves her, and anything that tends to disprove that, must be eliminated. The utter clarity of her position can help us recognize it in its (hopefully) milder forms, in our own lives.

And there are other drastic approaches, too regularly chronicled on the news. They go as far as holding the loved one prisoner or removing the beloved and oneself from the planet. In their extremity, they too highlight the ego's core logic. The message is, "Any world in which we are apart cannot stand. And no price is too high to pay, in order that there not be such a world."

with friends like these . . .

Maybe the toad's worst crime is lashing out at *other* people. But he has another approach, more frequent in most of our lives, that is very relevant to our chances of future love. That is when the romantic ego decides to turn inward and *protect its owner*. We have now arrived at what may be the most destructive thing that commonly happens to those of us who are injured by a breakup. It's the hardest to detect and admit, and it goes farthest to derail our future relationships. Learning to recognize it and overcome it is a huge step towards better love next time.

They praise us for the wrong things, and criticize us for the wrong things.

So what does the ego do? Stinging from the insult to our dignity, it vows that this will not happen again. No matter what, it won't allow anything that risks rejection. Like an over-protective brother, in its zeal to defend the heart's honor, the ego robs the heart of its freedom. It declares: "From now on, you will love only so far as you have the upper hand, the balance of power. At the first sign of trouble you will vamoose."

"Sorry, heart," it says. "You are grounded."

There are many of us walking around who have been crippled in this way. We are called "well defended." And we are, thanks to the wall and moat that the toad built around us. In many cases, we don't even know it. We go on for years, unaware of the way we've been compromised by one incident of pain.

So we choose lovers based on them not seeming like a threat. We don't get near people who might really challenge us. We seek the upper hand, or as they said on *Seinfeld*, we always want "more hand" than the other person. If we sense that the other person is gaining too much power, we play the goodbye card.

Above all, we avoid those who could really *know* us. Because they could do so much harm to our illusions. It's true that only they could appreciate us, and only they could free us from our shackles; but that's just the point, isn't it? Our jailer, the toad, loves our shackles. So we choose people who can't know us, and they praise us for the wrong things, and criticize us for the wrong things, and we can never get back into balance; because only real feedback can tame the toad.

If we do make a mistake and carelessly get involved with someone who really wants to see us and love us, we don't let them in. We keep them at a distance, keep them wanting more, and if they get too close, we resist. We stir up a fight, pick on some supposed inadequacy, find a way to drive them back. Or we run.

the demotion of the toad

So what is the way out?

The first challenge is to realize you *are* too well defended. The problem—what makes the ego so powerful—is that it works unconsciously in us most of the time; we don't even know why we are making all the right moves to elude intimacy and vulnerability, to keep the playing field tilted our way. The ego gets to control us without putting its cards on the table.

Examples of the thoughts that it may sneak into our brains:

- At this moment, this conversation is making me absolutely adore her, but I'll keep that to myself. It's better to play a little hard to get, and I hate mushy.

- He seems a little too happy with himself, a little too confident. Better knock him down a peg.

- I like spending time with her, but I have seen some flaws. I don't want to end up with a loser.

- He just looked at that girl walking by. Oh god, he's thinks she's hotter than me.

- She says she was just kidding around, but I see an insult in what she just said. Nobody does that to me. I'm going to give her grief about it.

- When it's meant to happen, the right person will come into my life. I'm certainly not going to make an *effort* to find somebody— that would make me look desperate.

- Casual relationships rule: you get the kicks without all the heavy crap.

- I really enjoy the chase and the challenge of someone who is hard to win. But once they give in and love me back, I just lose interest.[2]

---

2. This attitude might remind you of Bob the shipping clerk in Chapter 1.

How do we fight this sleight of hand? The answer is to bring the ego out in the open and force it to state its primitive little fight-or-flight argument. Then you can see what it is—a piece of lousy logic. So dispute that logic; demolish it. How? Let's see.

The ego says, "What happened to good old anger and resentment?"

The self: Okay, Mr. Toad, let's hear what you have to say. What is your point?

The ego: My point is simple. You got hurt, because you loved. So stop loving.

The self: Hey, anyone who loves exposes themselves to hurt, if only because real love is hurt by anything that injures the loved one, right up to death. Love expands your field of vulnerability beyond yourself. That's the <u>beauty</u> of it!

The ego: I didn't mean that kind of hurt. You got dumped! You got humiliated!

The self: Right, and that's all that matters to you.

The ego: You want to be rejected? You want to be found inadequate?

The self: Hey, I <u>am</u> inadequate—in some ways. In others I'm pretty cool. I don't mind if both are known. And anyway, your basic argument is wrong. I didn't get hurt because I loved someone. I got hurt because it didn't work out, this time.

The ego: Oh right, like it could work out with somebody else.

The self: Of course it could. There are <u>reasons</u> why it didn't work out this time. Maybe we just weren't right for each other. Maybe the timing wasn't right. Or maybe we just blew it. Maybe I blew it. I can figure these things out, if you would let me.

The ego: You're going to look at what really happened and own up to your part in it? That's sick. That smacks of humility. What happened to good old anger and resentment? What happened to winning?

The self: It isn't <u>about</u> winning. And by the way, you might want to own up to <u>your</u> part in what went wrong. I'm not sure you are innocent here. I seem to remember some pretty bad advice coming from you, back when there was still a chance. "Don't be brave, don't take risks, don't be honest." Oh, and your best one: "Don't let the power pass to the other person."

The ego: You're going to get us humiliated!

The self: You know what? I don't <u>care</u> if I get humiliated now and then. It's only hurt pride. And if I keep you under control, it won't be a big threat anyway.

A wounded ego is like a schoolyard bully—it rules with fear.
And what you have to say is: of course I'm afraid. But that won't keep me from trying. Because I'm not a coward like you.

It takes a kind of brutal self-honesty to admit that your pride has been demolished, that you've been brought low. But it's worth it. Because with that out of the way, you can revisit the history with clear eyes. You can be straight with yourself and fair to the others involved. You can take an honest inventory of your own behavior. You can figure out what really happened.

And that makes it possible to do better next time, as we'll see in Part Two, "Unlocking The Lessons of the Relationship."

I turn now to another thing that is part of many breakups—betrayal. The experience of being betrayed can do its own kind of harm, which will linger on if not dealt with. At the top of the betrayal marquee is a little thing called cheating. In the next two chapters we'll give that a thorough airing.

7

cheating's harm

how to defend against it

There's a sense of betrayal that happens when romantic love deserts us, whether a third party is involved or not.

That's because when someone is in love with you, part of that experience is being exalted above all others. When you are basking in that rarified esteem, it's a high beyond compare. And when that high is taken away, you feel not just deprived but betrayed. You want to say, "Didn't you really feel the way you said? If you did, why don't you feel that way now?" There is a feeling that you have been dishonored, and that you've been lied to.

I want now to explore the experience of betrayal, and in particular how to undo its dangerous after-effects. Our attempts to avoid being betrayed again can lead us in just the wrong direction when we pursue new love, so that we in fact encourage the trouble to recur and we use bad criteria to select our next partners.

Laptops, blackberries, and cell phones make it easier to hook up, and easier to conceal the fact that you are.

I'm going to use cheating as my case study, because it is probably the most telling example of betrayal and its dangers. Cheating is the most blatant violation of the promise of romantic love. That's because being in love, in full flame, is by its very nature infidelity-proof. When your partner admires you above all others—when you eclipse the rest of the field—they simply don't have any interest in being with someone else. This lack of interest, sometimes poetically described as being blind to everything but you, is one of the proofs that they really are in love. So when, later on, they evince an active desire to mix it up with someone else, this is unmistakable proof that the spell of love is on the wane. When they conceal what they're doing and you discover it after the fact, that is the final twist of betrayal's knife.

So let's look at this thing called cheating. It's almost trendy these days: it even has its own TV show. Both genders are doing it more than they used to, and women are catching up with men as doers. Modern technology has shown itself to be a two-edged romantic sword. The power of the Internet is a plus when we're looking for a good partner, but it becomes a minus once we're committed to someone, because it offers up such plentiful opportunities for straying. Laptops, blackberries, and cell phones make it easier to hook up, and easier to conceal the fact that you are doing so.

They also offer new options, such as:

- flirting by IM, e-mail, or text message

- carrying on an online romance

- cyber-sex.

There's no doubt that the prospect of hearing from someone (maybe a complete stranger) who is interested in you (and may not know you're attached) is highly entertaining. It's easy to get addicted to that stimulation.

But are these activities cheating, if they don't go as far as hooking up in the real world?

A good rule of thumb: if you have to hide it from your spouse, then the answer is probably yes.

And that points up the inherent contradiction in all cheating. *Why hide it if it's okay? And why do it if it's not?* There's a tacit admission of guilt in the very concealment. The cheater may answer: I'm not hiding it because *I* think it's wrong; I'm hiding it because my partner:

- might not be able to handle it

- might not approve of it

- might be hurt by it.

But if these potential feelings are respected so much, why not also honor the fact that your partner would almost certainly want to *know* what is going on? And what about the risk that they will find out later, and may be more hurt then than they would be now? Whatever you say about it, it's hard to call it straightforward.

Just to clarify: if at the dating stage you sleep with a second person without telling the first, that may not be cheating, and it isn't my subject here. I'll focus on the situation where two people in love have committed to a monogamous relationship, possibly with children, and at some point down the line the secret straying occurs.

People don't like being forced to scrap their own history.

I want to look at the whole process—how it happens, how the cheater thinks about it, what it does to the person cheated on, and how to save the future from its harmful influence. Then in the next chapter I'll look at another instructive subject—what cheating does to the cheater.

cheating as avoidance

To open up the subject of cheating, let's look at cheating as avoidance. Instead of dealing with the relationship they're in, some people start another one on the side.

Let's assume we're talking about a guy here. A number of things may be bothering him about his main relationship; but it would be a hassle to talk about them with his partner and then have to face the consequences of that and try to work through the issues. So he finds another avenue of relief. He finds a woman with whom he doesn't have problems yet, and drinks pleasure from her loving cup.

Now he has *two* things not to talk about with his partner. Which, in an opportune way, seem to balance each other out:

- *I don't have to talk to you about our problems, because I am getting relief from another woman.*

- *And I can't talk to you about the other woman, because that might stop her from providing the solution to our problems.*

It's a fine piece of juggling. And because a person who is getting relief is easier to get along with, it can happen that his partner, instead of suspecting what is going on, thinks things are improving.

So we get the two prerequisites of cheating: seeing someone else, and doing it secretly.

the theft of the past

Now the main purpose of this chapter is to look at the damage that results from a cheating-related breakup; but what about damage *before* that? As hinted earlier, it can be argued that as long as the partner doesn't know anything is going on, no damage has been done. Cheating is okay if you don't get caught.

Unfortunately that's incorrect on a couple of counts.

- **The energy you put into your secret lover, if applied to your main relationship, might have saved it. So you are robbing your main relationship of its blood supply.**

- **Unfaithfulness isn't ethically improved by the addition of lying.**[1]

When you lie to someone, you *are* damaging them. This will be more evident if we consider a point often made after cheating is discovered: "It isn't so much that you did it; it's that you *lied* about it."

What is the heart of this complaint? I think it's about being robbed of your past. "If you were lying to me about *that*, then *everything* between us was a lie." People don't like being forced to scrap their own history. To look back on months or years of time spent with someone and have to say that they were a charade, a macabre game, is a nasty fate. "The life I was living in good faith, you betrayed and made into a joke."

So while you are an undetected cheater, you are rigging the present with mines that will explode when the now is looked back on with knowledge. You are booby-trapping someone's life, so it won't hold up under future scrutiny.

You are making sure they will feel like a fool, when they find out.

---

1. This point is even more obvious if you also have to lie to the one you're cheating *with*, by pretending not to be attached. This kind of "double cheating" is also made easier by the Internet.

So they will say, "You thought me too dumb to detect the truth, and you thought me too insignificant to deserve to hear it. But other people knew about it (at least your lover did), and it was okay for them to know, and those who knew thought it was okay for me not to know. I guess you consigned me to a lower level."

At this point our old friend Bar Guy pipes up. (Yes, I seem to have wandered back into that bar. It's late afternoon and the sun is slanting in.) "Aren't you getting a little uptight about this?" he says, looking at my laptop screen. "There are cultures where cheating is no big deal. Look at France. They've got another institution, right alongside marriage. It's called having a mistress."

"Well, if the culture allows it, then it isn't cheating," I say. "So it isn't what I'm talking about. Especially if the wife or husband is in on the deal, and basically turns a blind eye to it."

What usually ends their fine arrangement is that they get caught.

A woman overhears us and approaches from a group whom I suspect to be college professors. She has black hair pulled back in a bun, and cool blue eyes. "If I may, you need a historical perspective," she says. "You have to bear in mind that in the old days, marriage wasn't primarily about love—let alone sex. It was about producing children. Economics, and for the higher-ups, politics too. A man wasn't trying to get emotional needs met by his spouse. Especially not romantic needs. So it was natural to look for that somewhere else."

"What—" Bar Guy says, "Are you saying mistresses are passé?"

Ms. Professor laughs. "I don't want to alarm you. In case you have one."

"I don't even have a wife," Bar Guy says. "I used to. Now I'm on my own."

"Do you like it that way?" she says.

"No . . . no, I don't. But it's hard to meet women. Especially here." He winks at me, and I'm wondering why. "They don't seem to ever come alone," he adds.

"Like me," she says. "I'm with that group over there. I should get back to them."

"You're adventurous," Bar Guy says. "You approached us. That's unusual."

Although I like his point, I can feel this discussion slipping its leash. I say to her, "I think you were about to say something about mistresses. You seem very knowledgeable; I wanted to hear what it was."

"Oh—of course. I'm a sociologist . . . " She looks at Bar Guy and laughs. "I was going to say that even in France I think you would get an argument from many women. Have you *been* to France?"

"Not really," he answers. "I've been to Quebec."

"Well I have a branch of my family in France," she says, "and I think my *cousines* would be surprised to hear that they are fine with their husbands having mistresses."

"I wouldn't want to surprise them," Bar Guy says.

Again I try to pull the dog in my direction. "So you're saying, today's couples expect marriage to be exclusive—even in France?" I ask her.

"That's exactly what I'm saying," Ms. P replies. "When you see your partner as your all-in-all, your soulmate *and* lover *and* friend— you're not going to like the idea of him turning to someone else. And that's the current template in the West."

"Sure," Bar Guy says, "but life isn't a fairy tale. You try for all that, maybe you try for too much. Sometimes the soufflé falls. Things change. People have needs."

"That's true," Ms. Professor says. "But missed shots don't make a target any less worthy." She sits down on the stool between me and

Bar Guy, looks at him. "Do you know a lot about soufflés?" she says.

"I'm a wizard with an egg," he answers.

"That's interesting. Are you a chef?"

Bar Guy smiles at her and says "Only in my spare time." Then he seems to remember that he was having a conversation with me.

"So, the point I was trying to make . . . " he says. "I read something about it in a book. It said even good people sometimes cheat on their way to their next relationship. Oh yeah, I think it was *your* book."

"You wrote a book?" Ms. P says. She seems genuinely surprised at the men you can meet in a bar.

But it's time for me to go.

I leave them leaning over their drinks.

the well-intentioned cheater

Bar Guy was right. Otherwise-honest people sometimes conceal a serious new relationship, at least while it's starting, from the person they're still married to. Let's say you've made a good effort in your marriage for years but find yourself basically miserable. You haven't *tried* to find a new lover, aren't looking for one, are willing to stick with the marriage to the bitter end. And then someone appears, and conversation occurs, and light breaks through. The thing is, at the beginning you may not know where that light is leading.

And one day on the road you realize you've crossed a border, even though there was no signpost to mark it. You've left behind the State of "It's too soon to tell my spouse about this, and anyway I don't know what it is yet" and you're now in the State of "I'm going to have to talk about this, and there is going to be a great upheaval."

Certainly, the truly honest thing to do would be to talk about it as soon as you know something—or better yet, to end one relationship before you even think about embarking on another. But it doesn't always go that way. So your spouse gets lied to, for a while.

the garden-variety two-timer

And of course there is another kind of situation, where unfaithful spouses aren't on the way to a new relationship at all, and don't have that justification for their behavior. In vast numbers of cases, they simply want some action on the side. Maybe the outside lover isn't available as a partner (maybe they're in a relationship they can't get out of); maybe kids are involved; or maybe our cheaters just have too much to lose. So they don't want to leave their spouse. If forced to choose, they would choose to stay in their marriage. But they don't *want* to choose: they want to have their cake and eat it too. (Or as I always thought this expression should read: eat their cake and have it too.)

Such persons are interested in permanent concealment, so they are unlikely to voluntarily let the cat out of the bag. What usually ends their fine arrangement is that they get caught. And then they get kicked out, and they lose a whole lot of things that they didn't want to lose. (More about them in the next chapter.)

the fallout

In either case, and regardless of who breaks it off or how it is discovered, the one cheated on is impacted in special ways, which can get in the way of future love. Let's see what they are, so we can counteract them.

The blotted diary. I spoke of this before: the ignominy of being forced to rewrite your own cherished history. It is like having kept a diary, and one day you find you have to take a black marker to it and cross out pages and pages of a life you valued. And the thing is, people aren't too careful when they are crossing out entries and tearing up photographs. They tend to throw out the good with the bad. The days that really were sunny, the absences that were innocent—they get trashed along with the rest. Everything is sullied; everything goes.

The longer-term result is cynicism, or even a loss of faith in the benign world that one used to take for granted—we'll look at that "fallen world" predicament, and one possible solution to it, in Chapter 9.

The return of the toad. Being rejected and dumped is bad enough; being left for another is worse; and being *lied to* about being left for another may be the worst of all—in terms of the offence taken by the kingly ego. We have seen how the toad reacts to this: how he takes control and shoulders the heart aside, so a person becomes too well defended to be able to love. All that applies to the cheating situation, in spades.

> It's risky to judge honesty by whether someone *says* he is honest.

Inability to trust. But the toad isn't always the star of the show. People with properly trimmed egos also get cheated on and hurt. And a major consequence is the loss of the ability to trust.

It is disquieting how easily we humans fall into generalizing about the other gender, *based on one person.* We become bitter; we take a jaundiced view of all men or all women. We think we know that they are all liars, all users, all betrayers. This may be the result of simple hurt, but it's a child's response, a simplistic retreat from other people. I think it's especially likely to happen when our trusted partner turned out to be brutal and nasty, and seemed to enjoy hurting us. "I get it," we say. "All men/women are snakes in the grass, just waiting to reveal their evil nature. But they won't get *me!*" Unfortunately this prophecy turns out to be only too true. In the smugness of victory we find isolation.

The quest for Mr. Won't-leave. Another troubling legacy of cheating —the obsessive search for someone who *can* be trusted.

I have had a number of requests for advice through the whymrright.com Web site, along the following lines:

> My boyfriend/husband left me for a younger/older woman, whom he'd been seeing on the sly for six months. I want to find a new guy, but I've almost lost my belief that <u>any</u> man can be trusted. So I have a plan; please tell me if it is any good.
>
> On my new personal ad on a major dating site, I stress in my profile that the man I'm looking for must be honest and loyal, a good person, as I am—no cheaters or players!
>
> Also, my last guy had certain characteristics.
>
> • he was ten years younger/older than I am;
> • he drove a really flashy sports car/didn't even own his own car
> • he was a lawyer/a carpenter
> • he lived with other men/lived with his parents.
>
> So I have vowed not to have anything to do with any guys who have any of these features, because I've been burned once.
>
> Will this plan work?

My answer has been: no, it won't work.

It isn't a good idea for this woman to try desperately to find The Type of Man Who Won't Cheat.

Because the characteristics she will use to *identify* this type—to ferret him out from the vast unwashed mass of men—are deceptive.

Mr. Honest. Suppose she focuses on his inner character, on his honesty. Then (especially online) she will probably have to rely on his words to announce him. That method is a snare in which she is likely to catch herself. A woman who hangs out a sign saying she is looking for honesty is likely to attract dishonest men: they will quickly sense that she has been deceived before, and that she is sensitive and vulnerable on this point. In their eyes this means she can be deceived again. All they have to do is talk about honesty and integrity and faithfulness and loyalty, and how their whole life has been dedicated to these virtues.

Most men realize that they have not always been wholly honest, and will admit it when pressed. Men who boast about being perfectly honest, may be conning you. Now am I saying that honesty isn't a virtue? Oh god no. I think it is one of the *highest* virtues, and may be the last bastion against life's most dangerous temptations. (There are many occasions when we know we could get away with something, but we don't do it, for the simple reason that it would require a lie. When people tell the truth even though it puts them at a disadvantage, they are showing humanity at its best.)

But I think it's risky to judge honesty by whether someone *says* he is honest. Especially if you're looking at an online ad, not at a person. A better way to assess honesty is to observe someone's actual behavior over time; see if he is willing to criticize himself; get to know him. People tend to be more honest when they think they will be believed and understood and accepted, so it's nice if a lot of that goes on too.

The problem, even if you find a truthful man, is that honesty alone won't keep a person from falling for someone else, or from concealing it for a while. We'll see in a moment what else is needed to prevent that outcome.

Mr. Won't-Leave. My advice example illustrates another troubled response: fixating on *external* features of the person who left you for someone else. In a kind of superstitious or magical reasoning, the victim tells herself that whatever the last guy was, that's what to avoid. *The guy who dumped me was a carpenter ten years older than me who didn't own his own car, so if I stay away from those things I'll be safe.* So *all* of the characteristics of the guy who cheated on her become red flags for the future, regardless of whether they had anything to do with his cheating! It's kind of like the ancient Pict who noticed that a hailstorm came after he ate an apple, so he never ate one again.

The root of both mistakes is believing that there is a certain inherent type of person, "the type who won't leave." If you look for that, you are looking for a phantom. The truth is that *any* man, or *any* woman, may leave if they don't have enough reason to stay. So if you want a partner who will hang around, and will make *you* want to hang around, what you should be looking for is *someone with whom you have so much going that either of you would be nuts to leave the other.* That's right, the key to people not cheating is not their character so much as the quality of the rapport they have. Otherwise known as compatibility. Find a man that you have a lot in common with, in a lot of areas. For example, values, career goals, sense of humor, sexuality, intellect, entertainment . . . the list goes on.[2] A man like this will be too engrossed in you to think he could do without you, and you will feel the same.

The experience of being left for another, and lied to about it, is one of the toughest ones that life hands out. It takes time to recover from the blow, but you are more likely to recover if you are aware of its potential after-effects and consciously resist them. We've done some of that work in this chapter, and we'll do a lot more in what follows. The next chapter will provide perspective by looking at the cheater's

---

2. Compatibility is discussed in detail in Part Two of *Why Mr Right Can't Find You.* I'll explore it in relation to the lessons of the past in Chapter 15 of this book.

own blues. Chapter 9 will delve more into the spiritual side of healing, which certainly can alleviate betrayal, and Part Two of this book will look into the relationship itself, in ways that will help.

Meanwhile keep this positive goal in your back pocket: instead of being crippled by the experience of being left for another, use it as motivation: redouble your efforts to find a partner who is really a good match for you.

8
the cheater's blues

*I*f you've been cheated on, one thing that can help you recover is to consider that the cheater often does not emerge unscathed. You can also gain perspective by looking at both sides of a story, as we did with the process of breaking up. So let's enter for a while into the cheater's fate.

Now it's obvious that garden-variety two-timers, when they get nabbed, can lose a great deal. They may be ejected from a whole life that they didn't want to leave: may lose partner, friends, good name and various other assets.[1] But even what I called the "well intentioned" cheater—the one who stumbled accidentally onto a new relationship, and left voluntarily—can sustain serious losses.

And of those losses, the ones that interest me right now are emotional and spiritual.

So here are a few reflections on the surprising price paid by the unfaithful.

---

1. I'll discuss the whole topic of the assets that are lost in breakups in Chapter 10, "Surviving and Recouping".

the lover's reward

Unfortunately, when you cheat you draw your lover, even if he is un-attached, into the same now-tarnished universe that you share with your spouse.

Firstly, when you "lie" with the other man, he is drawn into the same lie that you are telling. And from his point of view, he is betray-ing another guy. Usually he doesn't hear that guy's side of the story, and he may not want to, because we can more easily ignore feelings that we don't directly witness. The people we interact with are real, and everybody else somehow isn't.

Secondly, cheating inadvertently demonstrates the same thing to your lover that it will eventually demonstrate to your spouse, if and when they learn the truth. It embeds in your lover's mind a perfect movie of your ability to stray and lie about it. He now has road-tested your unreliability, as if to prepare himself for the time when he will be the one flung out of the car.

The general effect of both these points is that the one you cheat *with* may have more trouble in the future trusting either gender, and in particular, you.

And that's your first problem: you're responsible for that.

the cheater

Now what are the direct effects on the cheater?

Just to spread blame around evenly (and to keep the pronouns simple), let's make it a guy this time. Assuming he has half a heart, he is going to have a truckload of ills.

Beginning when the affair is still a secret, he will feel guilty. When he is with his lover, he'll feel guilty because he has to leave her too soon. When he is with his partner, he'll feel guilty because he is holding a secret she doesn't know. This will be especially bad when his partner is behaving really well, when she is being loving or playful or in other ways trusting. Even though she isn't damaged yet in her own eyes, she *is* damaged in his, and this is an awful thing for him to carry around, a strange kind of sad horror. He may also feel weak and cowardly, because he hasn't told her, because she doesn't deserve such treatment.

And after the split hits the fan and it's over, he'll have plenty more reasons for guilt, especially if there are children involved.

> The actions we choose in our lives make it more likely that we will choose similar actions in the future.

Then there's strayer's remorse. This happens when the blush comes off the new rose and suddenly a fella realizes that the old rose was rather nice. The old rose didn't have so many thorns as this tangled new one, and it had a pretty amazing red color that, come to think of it, endured through the years and reblushed itself often.

The grief of a man who sits in a parking lot in the rain because he doesn't want to go home to his new love and can never go home to his old love, is a fine thing to contemplate.

The thing is, the person he wants to return to has done no wrong. Like a screen idol who died young, she remains unsullied forever; she reigns in the memory and is burnished by the rag of his own mistake. No distance is so cold and unconsoling as the distance one created oneself.

How about trust? Oh yes, the liar's blues are all about trust.

Deep down, the poor rogue has to doubt himself. Every time he gets involved with a new woman, he has to wonder in his bones, "Do I really mean it? Am I going to leave this one too? Do I buy my own line of malarkey?"

In his own eyes he has become a slightly shoddy product, a tarnished gold piece.

Plus he has begun to carve a groove in which he now can more easily skate. The term "karma" is often taken to mean that what goes around comes around, and the guilty will be punished, if not in this life (where it seems a lot of them thrive), then in the next. But there is a more profound, and more chillingly plausible, sense of karma.

That is, that the actions we choose in our lives make it more likely that we will choose similar actions in the future. If you drink alcohol in a moment of despair, you make it more likely that you will drink again, and deeper, when you're down. If you shy away from the thing you really want to do, if you balk because it is too scary, you are more likely to chicken out in the face of the next challenge. If you compromise your integrity in little things, you are more likely to compromise it in big ones.

If a man leaves a worthy woman for someone else, if he breaks someone's trust, he is more likely to see himself as *someone who does that kind of thing*, and that will make him less convincing in the nobler role he may want to play. Less convincing to himself, and therefore less convincing to the one he may need most to impress, the worthy woman down the line that he is most desperate to win.

If he can't trust himself, imagine another problem his karma may bring him in the future—how is he going to trust any woman?

Lastly, in our inventory of the cheater's problems, we can't neglect our old friend the ego. The ego may well have seconded the cheating. Cheating avoids the risk of commitment. And it resets the meter of intimacy, by which I mean that a new person doesn't know you yet, and you escape from the growing knowledge of the old person. All of which the toad applauds. (*To be known*, it likes to say, *is to imperil one's dignity.*)

So at the big meeting, the toad voted for making a break and seducing a new person; and therefore the toad may be feeling his oats, or his dead flies, and may get a little swelled up. He may congratulate himself on having the power to hurt other people, the blade to cut a wide swath through the trusting population. He may whisper in his owner's ear: you are the Lothario, you cain't be tamed by no woman, you can do as you please. "Guard your daughters," he croaks in the night to all the farmers whose houses lie by his swamp.

Then we get a small-time felon, a man who cheated, who is no longer in charge of his own life. He has a new, badder boss: a toad dressed as a buccaneer.

And if anything is bad karma, that is.

9

losing your religion

a world gone wrong, and a way out

What an amazing thing we try for, when we launch a serious relationship. We're picking one person, out of all the people in the world, to form a couple with, and around that couple we hope to structure our whole life—domestic, emotional, social, and financial, often including children. It's amazing we ever have the temerity to place such a bet. The only way to do that is to really *believe* in it. It's like founding your own religion. The belief in your partner becomes your central dogma.

So when that platform fails, when suddenly you find that this person isn't going to be the one after all, the whole edifice of your life seems to slip, as if it has lost its moorings. There's a sense that the whole universe has gone crazy, has tilted madly. The world isn't right anymore. Your coordinates of truth have been knocked askew.

We end up in a world that doesn't feel crazy, but in fact it may be crazy.

Even when you instigated the breakup, this can be true: your belief in the universe that the two of you represented, is gone. So how do you believe in anything?

We can't live very long with that first crazy feeling, so after a while we have to erect a new belief system to substitute for the old one. And that's when things get tricky, because the new system has to remove anything that may have led to the collapse of the old one. And the easiest way to do that is to get rid of the parts that made hope possible in the first place.

We end up in a world that doesn't *feel* crazy—that's what makes us more comfortable there—but in fact it may *be* crazy.

In order to understand its insanity, we need to look harder at the madness that led to it, and still infects its timbers.

That initial feeling of disorientation, that tilting feeling, which follows a breakup. I'm going to offer some comparisons here, to capture the sense of unreality, the surreal sensation, that is so hard to deal with. What is that experience like?

It's like what a child feels when her parents divorce. *I lie in my bedroom at night—or is it still my bedroom? It is on some nights . . . I don't feel safe. The walls that kept the night away, they don't feel so solid anymore. The big world can get me. The grownups had my back, so I could be a kid. Now I'm not so sure. I don't feel the same way about them anymore. Or myself.*

It's like what an adult feels when his parents die. Again, the buffer is gone. *There's no one between me and the grim reaper. I'm next on his list.*

Moving even closer to religion, it's like what one feels when one's friend is struck down by a senseless accident. This is when people tend to lose their faith. They say, "The god I believed in wouldn't have let this happen."

It's like having the world's best job, and one Friday morning they come to your office and they tell you to collect your things—just your personal effects—and they escort you out of the building. You didn't suspect a thing. You were doing a good job. Your position was solid. This can't be happening.

It's a little like watching those towers come down. (I'm referring to the disbelief of seeing the physical structures collapse, and not the other sorrows of that grievous day.)

It's like that moment in the movie *The Truman Show*, when Truman Burbank (Jim Carrey) is driving through his sunny town and his car radio accidentally picks up the secret patter of those who control and shape his whole life. His world—wife, friends, job, everything—is a clever illusion created by a TV studio, and for a crazy moment that illusion slips, making him doubt everything he knows.

I use these examples to conjure the sense of dislocation, of disconnection, the feeling of being lost in space, that can engulf you when the relationship you based everything on disappears, and the two people who said they loved each other, walk away from each other.

Things that were always true, aren't true anymore.

- You don't believe that other people are basically good, or that you understand them. Especially members of the opposite sex.

- You don't trust your own goodness; it doesn't seem obvious anymore that you *deserve* to be happy with someone.

- You doubt that any couples are really happy.

- You doubt your own judgment. You've always been a good judge of character, and in this instance you certainly did your very best to pick out a fine partner. And now it's all gone to hell, so what does that say about your discernment?

- In particular, you doubt your own ability to detect fraud. You keep sifting through all the clues that were in the situation. All the signs that something was wrong. Apparently you could stare right at them and think they were fine. "I don't know the real thing from the fake," you tell yourself. "I don't know a healthy relationship from a travesty. Maybe they're all fake, all travesties."

So you conclude that nothing is what it seems. "What a fool I was," you think. "I took everything at face value; I was so naïve."

You walk out the front door and the street feels different. Everything seems worthy of a certain suspicion. The tree may drop a limb on you if you walk blithely beneath it. The grass may contain a wasp's nest. The people on the sidewalk are up to something. The cars all carry some smug secret, some mockery that may be at your expense.

How did you ever believe in love?

John Donne wrote a poem once in which he said, "And now goodmorrow to our waking souls, which watch not one another out of fear." And now you think, wouldn't that be nice, to look at someone without any trepidation. But that's exactly what you no longer know how to do.

You've lost your innocence.

I don't mean naivety here—that's a good thing to lose—I mean a deeper thing. A bad breakup can seriously affect your spiritual health, for a long time. It can mire you in what some traditions would call a "fallen world." I want to unmask that impaired place, and to point a way out. To do that I'm going to walk us through a spiritual "landscape," slightly exaggerated to reveal its true nature. That will help us see it for what it is, which is the first step in breaking free.

why a fallen world is a bad place to live

A fallen world is a seductive place.

It is a secure place, where you can count on things being the way you expect them to be. Namely, mediocre. No surprises here.

It's a safe place: you are not called on to take any serious risks.

And it's an amiable place: there's plenty of company. Maybe a lot of them are disillusioned, cynical, defeated. But they're nice to have around, because they agree that there never was any hope and what happened to you was inevitable. It happened to them too.

It's a place where a constant dull pain is considered normal, and that's why painkillers are considered life's greatest invention.

A fine world, this fallen one, except for one problem. It was constructed out of insanity. The builder (your psyche) took the madness, the sense of nauseating disorientation that struck you when your relationship first fell apart, and found a way to contain it, to shift the crushing weight of it, by spreading it out, graying it over, extending it through time.

Your old beliefs that we listed, the ones that trembled in the balance when the first shock hit, are missing now. They are nowhere to be found in the new world. It is sustained by the opposite principles. If you strip off the façade of its buildings, you will find support timbers that say things like: *All men are bad. You are unworthy of love. All couples are miserable. Your judgment is faulty.* The earlier beliefs, now replaced, were what made love possible. This new world has taken the doubts that beset you in your stricken moment, and has enshrined them as dusty law.

The main enterprise of a fallen world is the avoidance of reality. That can be done in so many ways. Most of them involve addictive behavior. What you want is to forget the positive vision you once had, and how awful it was when it fell apart. Addictions are really good for that purpose. Everything from sleep to drugs to alcohol to TV will pitch in and do its part.

It's a world where sins of omission reign supreme. (Sins of commission require too much passion.) You think of something to say at work—something that could solve a problem—but it might make waves, so you don't. You see someone interesting across a room, but they might not like you so you don't smile. You shy away, shy away, close the blind, close the door, close your mind.

Your life becomes a web of habits that forms a shroud over feelings that are too painful to face. And memories that are easier ignored.

You've lost your innocence.

the way out

Is there any way to get it back?

Again, spiritual traditions have an interesting answer. They say, a god has to die. According to the ancient Egyptian mystery religion, a man-god has to die on a tree, and be reborn, and then the rain will come again and the crops will grow. The waste land will turn green.

> Devote yourself to the things you would believe in if the world were right again.

If you take that as a metaphor, it tells us what has to happen within your soul, when you are in this predicament. Something has to die in your soul, so that something can be reborn.

Which leads to a rather surprising prescription for what ails you, when you have lost your heart's spark.

That is to concentrate on the parts of your being that are most screamingly idealistic, most prone to hope—and follow those impulses. Devote yourself to the things you would believe in if the world were right again.

Dedicate yourself to others. Give some form of service to help the needy or the suffering. Or the planet. Fight for a losing cause that has merit. (People who did that are the reason some of those causes eventually won.) Take the dream you have neglected for years— the thing that scares you the most—and go for it. Get rid of the things (and people) in your life that pander to discouragement and cynicism. Say, "If the world has given up, that is just one more reason why I won't."

It may not be time yet to try for love. So try for something else, something that isn't a need of your own. Something you believe in. Then a strange thing will happen.

You will start to meet people who don't fit in a fallen world. That is because you will be leaving it behind.

10

 surviving and recouping

$\mathcal{I}$n the last chapter I described a kind of spiritual fall that can happen when a relationship fails. The soul can falter and retreat, and hardly know it has done so. But there's a more external fall that is also possible, and sometimes we don't defend ourselves properly against it. A person's whole darn lifestyle can be threatened.

So a warning needs to be sounded. It says: a storm is coming, there is danger, so grab the supplies you need, put up the plywood and get inside. Don't trifle with this thing; don't do anything reckless or careless. Your first duty is to survive.

When love comes tumbling down, that perfect storm can sweep a lot of assets away. In Chapter 2, I talked about some of the emotional benefits coupling confers on a human being, which are lost when love goes belly-up. They were not the whole story. When a solid relationship comes apart, you can lose a whole truckload (or U-Haul load) of valuable stuff—some material things and some less so—and this situation needs to be dealt with.

There's a good-news side though: what you lose is relative to how much you had. If before the breakup, the relationship was pretty lousy and it was obvious to you that its assets had slipped in value, then you won't have lost as much.[1] But if the relationship was still good or *seemed good to you*, that's a different story.

I'm going to list some advantages that a truly healthy couple has. You can look at this list in several ways, depending on your situation. If you had these advantages—if things were going that well before the breakup—then this chapter will be about how to minimize and repair their loss. If, however, you were in the situation I mentioned a moment ago, and a lot of these benefits were missing from your relationship, you can take heart from the fact that you didn't lose as much, and more important, you can take this inventory as a yardstick to employ when next you embark on love. As you're getting to know the new relationship, check to see that these good things are in the offing.

Imagine a cliff house, built on four pillars. The Four Pillars of Couplehood. As a member of a couple, you get to live on a higher level, with the cruel sea crashing far below, distant enough to be picturesque. What are these four things that support your platform?

1. Financial advantages: two earners in the household

2. Teamwork, where the duo can solve problems and make plans better than either could alone

3. Recognition and support: the feeling that you matter to someone, and the feeling that someone has your back

4. Physical health; lack of loneliness; mental health.

---

1. In Chapter 13 we'll look at this brighter scenario. In some ways the last relationship may have been doing you more harm than good, in which case there are unexpected benefits of being alone again. But first we need to deal with the danger.

Let's talk about these things, and then we'll see what can be done about their loss.

THE FOUR PILLARS OF COUPLEHOOD

1. financial advantages

What's the big advantage of a two-earner household? Couldn't it be argued that whichever partner makes more money, will actually *lose* on the deal? If Samantha makes sixty grand a year and Sam makes forty, then the income per person of their union is $50,000, which is a drop of $10,000 for Samantha. One loses and the other gains. Sounds like a wash at best.

> It only takes one kitchen, for the lucky couple who don't mind being jostled now and then while making toast.

Then why, for decades, have studies said that married people are better off financially? Some answers that have been offered:

- They earn more; that is, spouses each bring home more bacon than they would if they'd stayed single. This was supposed to be because people had more time for their careers and put more into them. Recent studies have disputed this, pointing out that women often cut back on their jobs and earn less, especially when children arrive, and men's increases are not that big.

- They plan and save better. This seems to be a fact, and a very important one. Because married couples *believe* in the long term, they plan for it. They have the incentive of the team: they are willing to make sacrifices, to budget, to save and invest for the future and for their kids' futures. To put it another way, people grow up and watch their pennies.

- They can live for less, thanks to what are called "economies of scale". This may be the heart of the matter. One house may not cost any more per month than two apartments—more likely less. Two people (and their kind relatives) are more likely to be able to swing that down payment, and thereby ascend to the next plateau. With both of them commuting to work every day they may not *see* much of that dream house, but it's still a house. The thing is, it only takes one kitchen, for the lucky couple who don't mind being jostled now and then while making toast. One living room, one dining room. Two people don't need twice as many rooms as one. Two people don't need twice as much food, or electricity, or a lot of other necessities—so what is called their "needs-adjusted income" is now higher than before.

What about couples who cohabit (live together unmarried)? These flouters of tradition were once thought to be at a disadvantage as compared to folks in wedded bliss, but recent studies have called this into question, especially as regards how much they earn. Apparently cohabiters and married couples *both* do better than single people.[2]

The bottom line here is that the dissolution of a couple can spell real financial hardship, an abrupt slip to a lower ledge on the cliff side. And the partner who gained the most in the union (usually the lower wage-earner) may lose the most in the fall.

2. teamwork

This word means much more than cold finances might suggest. In a thousand ways, big and small, two people working together can

---

2. "Gender Differences in the Marriage and Cohabitation Income Premium," by Audrey Light of Ohio State University, pages 21-22. This interesting article is well worth Googling if you want to explore the subject more.

avoid calamities and bring about better results. Their combined talents can handle a lot more challenges than either could alone. One person trying to change an outdoor floodlight might end up with a cracked skull; two people doing it are more likely to brace the ladder properly. They're also more likely to nag each other into replacing the bulb in the first place, which then prevents their visiting dancer friend from breaking her leg on the bottom step and bringing a massive lawsuit.

Not to mention land subsidence. With two people you've got a better chance that one partner will notice the hole appearing next to the front porch, and the other will figure out that it's being caused by rain spouting off the awning, and one of the two will know how to take the damn thing down, thus avoiding a flood in the basement that could wreck the carpet and the entertainment center.

Before this turns into a commercial for Home Depot, let me say that two people can figure out how to do the taxes and plan a lavish meal for ten and launch a new business and handle an aging parent and buy the right car and get the brakes fixed before it's too late.

3. recognition and support

We lose a lot of the spotlight when we take the big demotion into adulthood. Our society tries very hard to create the sense in a child that she is special and that every highlight of her life is worth attending and camcording.

But never fear: we do eventually find our way to that place of nonrecognition; it awaits us in adulthood. Those of us not lucky enough to be big cheeses at our jobs find ourselves in the day, not so important anymore, occasionally winning praise or censure, but much of the time not arousing any notable emotion in our co-workers. Then we drive home in an empty vehicle, and in the evening we watch famous people on TV. It is possible to live a life of impressive invisibility.

Being part of a couple allays that. Someone notices little things like whether you get home, what you eat, how you sleep, how you smell, whether you are sick, whether you are okay. (We're transitioning into *support* now.) Your presence is an expected part of their day; the morning just wouldn't be the same without you. Your attendance is called for.

You're back on the marquee of life.

Someone wants to know where you are. If something goes wrong, you are likely to be found. If you throw your lower back into spasm while picking up a sock and can't get off your bed for five days, someone will be there to bring you food and an empty bucket, and meds. In that case, they literally have your back.

Our brains are addicted to interruption.

Someone knows if you get a promotion. They may even know if it's your birthday. Someone thinks you are good looking today. Someone wants to kiss you.

Someone is there to vent to. What fun.

Recognition has a downside too. Except it turns out to be mostly an upside. There are things you might drift into, if you were living alone (or at least I might). But somehow, you just can't do them while another person is monitoring you, even if that person is not especially nosy or critical or interfering. It's harder to watch TV when there's nothing on, harder to eat the corn chips and pesto you really crave late at night, harder to lie around doing nothing on a Saturday afternoon. Harder to drink Jack Daniels just because you're bored. It's also harder to be bored. It's harder to let dirty dishes pile up, harder to avoid the minor challenge of preparing nutritious meals.

Being seen: what an imposition!

And support: what a burden. If you are living with somebody else, then you spend a lot of your time *caring* about somebody else. Wanting them to do well, wanting to make sure nothing happens to them, worrying that they may be struggling or having trouble—wanting to make sure they don't get defeated. When the other person is thriving, you take joy in that.

Oddly enough, caring about somebody else is good for your health. It's the best thing for us humans. Nurturing makes us feel . . . nurtured. It lightens the unbearable burden of "I". (Okay, we all need to be self-absorbed some of the time, and creative types claim it's most of the time, but even artists can be saved from insanity by having to worry about somebody else.)

The reason couples live longer is that people who are caring for somebody else live longer.

The extreme form of that involves children. The closest many of us ever get to being truly unselfish is when we find that we are somebody's parent. We will give to our children what we would otherwise never give. What we receive *from* them, not in return but simply because they can't help it, is of course worth much more: they put a stop to the strange amnesia that afflicts grown-ups, who should maybe be called "grown-downs" when you consider that we have forgotten most of what is thrilling and giddy and hilarious and astounding about life—we have forgotten how to be young.

4. physical health; lack of loneliness; mental health

These things are not always easy to separate.

"You look pale," your partner says. "Oh, you're clammy."

And you say, oh god, I am. I think I got a chill. Or I caught a bug.

"Maybe it was when you were on the plane."

Yeah, that must have been it.

"You better get under the blanket. I'll make you some tea."

Even more important than helping someone with their symptoms, is helping them figure out what ordinary, familiar, unscary thing must have caused them, and helping them decide that this exact same thing has happened before and it was alright last time. That alleviates the stress and fear, which then forces the illness to wage a solitary battle, minus its two favorite allies.

Speaking of mental health, it isn't easy trying to aid someone who is suffering from depression or anxiety—or garden-variety sadness or disappointment. But it's a job easier done by one person than by no one. Sometimes you have to leave a person alone; you can't comfort them, you can't coach them. Sometimes they need your immediate intervention, they need to be held up so they won't slump to the floor, need to be told that this isn't the end of the world and they can't let some alleged friend incapacitate them.

The best way to deal with what has been lost is to regain it in a different form.

So-called illness can turn out to be something more mundane. Insomnia can be the latest disguise of a rascal called "Late Night Snacking"; restless leg syndrome can be an alias of "Doesn't Go for Walks Enough." And depression—it may be a cloak worn by loneliness. Years can go by during which a person doesn't get a whole lot done, because he is too depressed to try. Making an effort requires a little optimism, and he doesn't have any. That could be because he is alone. Some people do fine on their own. Some don't. Especially people who have known what it was not to be alone, and liked it.

We don't always notice it, but when we are part of a couple, we correct each other in a multitude of tiny ways. I don't mean "correct" as in correcting someone's grammar. I mean moving the rudder slightly so that the boat stays on course. When someone has tried their best to express something but didn't quite nail it, there are various ways that you can help them hit their target. One is to nod, signifying that you understand. That may make them smile and say it better. Another is to paraphrase it for them. So, by quiet or eloquent listening, you help them vent a truth, and sometimes that is the difference between life sinking and life sailing on.

Listening is just one of many ways in which we gently lead our partners towards mental health, and away from discouragement, isolation, and dysfunction. But I bring it up and dwell on it here, because it is among the most priceless and neglected gifts two people can bestow on each other. Waiting quietly and with attention for someone to complete their thought may be the most endangered conversational activity. It isn't easy; in fact it's way too hard for a lot of us. Today's programming is rapid-cut, zing and move on. Our brains are addicted to interruption. But to listen is to nurture.

reproduction

Nature's deepest reason for having couples in the first place is, of course, reproduction. Even though a single parent can raise children, and in today's world you don't even have to have sex to conceive a child, it remains true that the optimal situation for child-rearing is a loving, prosperous couple. And all four of the pillars we've just looked at, help make this true. Successful reproduction may well be thought of as their biggest payoff, and if you were headed there with someone, it's very bad news to have them drop out of the plan.

replacing the pillars

It's pretty obvious, having inventoried these assets that a lone human being finds in a couple, that being thrown back into the world without them could be a shock to the system.

At this point a couple of temptations may arise. They must be resisted.

- You may observe your ex with great interest, and he may get away with all sorts of stuff that you therefore think *you* should be able to get away with too. Maybe he dives right into a rash new relationship; or that's what he already did. Maybe he quits his job and cashes in his retirement. Maybe he leaves town and goes to live with his uncle in Paducah. Don't use your former partner as a role model. Just because he does reckless things in the throes of freedom, doesn't mean you have to. What works for him—or crashes and burns for him—may not work for you. Your best bet is to hang tough, hang on, and keep a firm grip on your resources until the smoke clears.

- You may want to get revenge on him by the martyr strategy of hurting yourself. Don't. That gambit always backfires.

The best way to deal with what has been lost is to regain it in a different form. In fact, your job after a breakup (rather than letting yourself be knocked off your pins) is to *replace each of the four pillars as best you can in your new situation*, or at least protect yourself from further attrition in each of those areas.

Financial. Take care of your job. Hang on to your own possessions and don't throw them away (or concede them to your ex) in a fit of pique. Find ways to keep your housing to a reasonable cost— look into a shared situation if necessary.

Teamwork. If the main team you were part of has dissolved, form a new, wider team. Most of us know someone who is smart about almost any type of problem that may show up on our plate today. So enlist help from the right friend, buy them a drink or a meal, and add them to your team. Get even better advice than you had before.

Join groups who share your objectives. There are amazing resources online these days. For example, the Meetup.com network is a noble and prolific resource: you can find other people in your region who are pursuing almost anything, from canoeing to jewelry making to writing to dancing . . . so get with them, make some new friends, gain allies in the things you do and renew your interest in things you dropped along the way.

Recognition and Support. You may feel embarrassed by what has happened. You may prefer that your friends and family not observe you. If some of them are too intertwined with your ex or too invested in what might have been, maybe you do need to steer clear of them. But don't turn away from the ones whose only faults are that they care about you and can see clearly.

As I said earlier, you do not want to go this alone. It makes it too big. You want your robe of misery to be trimmed down to size by the strange combination of caring and not-caring-as-much that we prize in other people. Their selfishness gives them objectivity, and their affection gives them empathy—a potent combination. Again, seek out someone you can confide in and be honest with. Find someone new or someone professional if you need to; tell your story and let it become an ordinary piece of fact among other known facts. Then it'll be easier to deal with.

Having said that, there's another front in this war. *You need to grow the part of your life that has nothing to do with your ex.* Other people can help you do that. They can give you the ordinary validation and encouragement that we all need in our emotional diets, they can make demands on you and ask for help with their own miseries, and they can lead you back to laughter and entertainment, and on to new vistas and new plans. External friendships often get short-changed by couples; so now is your chance.

Remind yourself that a good friend is better than a bad partner.

Health. Do what makes you healthy, physically and mentally. Do what you may have been neglecting. Eat the good things your mate didn't like. Walk or run. Meditate.

Staying healthy includes honoring your negative feelings, by giving them a hearing and by getting someone else to listen to them. Express whatever sadness and hurt and anger are coursing through you, so they don't get bottled up and turn their guns inward.

You'll go through stages. At times the past will seem to swamp you; maybe it has to for a while. At other times you'll be able to shrug it off and take positive steps of the sort I've mentioned. So don't try to turn into Ms. Positive all the time. Cut yourself some slack, but don't forget to protect the things you haven't lost.

Take care of yourself in every way—health, social life, job, home. Ask for and get help.

Survive long enough to come up for air and feel your own powers of recuperation. So that when you look around with clearing eyes, you will find that you have a support system; you didn't let it fall to pieces.

Buy yourself enough time to get on the comeback trail.

Survive.

That concludes my survey of the aftermath of a breakup. We've inventoried the effects and have looked at ways of containing, controlling, coping with, and starting to heal them. We've separated a broken heart from a wounded ego and have seen how to deal with both; we've treated the cheater's devastation. We've walked through the fallen world where innocence is lost, and begun to find a way out, and we've worked on everyday survival.

So the wounded soldier we started with is beginning to be in better shape. That means it's time for stage two of the process. We need to figure out how you got into that battle in the first place, and why you lost. That way you can get into a better one next time, and win. (The enemy, as I said, being the forces that make relationships fail.)

So let's cast our eyes back to the relationship that didn't last, and ask the interesting question, what went wrong? How did one get mixed up in such an ill-fated venture? And how did it go so awry?

We want to avoid the same thing happening in the future.

So it's time to probe the past.

PART

II

UNLOCKING THE LESSONS OF THE RELATIONSHIP

11

rebound logic

what happens if we don't listen to the past

*B*efore we turn to the relationship that went wrong and start to investigate what it has to tell us, it may be a good idea to give ourselves an extra shot of motivation.

People say, "Life is tough, but I prefer it to the alternative." A witty way of saying it's not so hard to shoulder life's load when you consider the other option.

That's also the case with examining the past. It's a challenging thing to do: it requires honesty, courage, patience and fairness. But the alternative is much worse. If you don't do it, you end up caught in a thing I call

> **When you're on the rebound, your new relationship isn't about itself; it's about the old one.**

rebound logic. And that is the worst, most botched-up version of being governed by the past. It's the way not to go. By seeing why, we'll understand better what we're trying to do in Part Two of this book.

Our culture warns us about love on the rebound. "Don't get involved with him," they say, "he's still reverberating from his last girl who dumped him." The (correct) implication is, whatever happens between you and him won't be real, because he's still in the grip of the previous disaster.

When you're on the rebound, your new relationship isn't about itself; it's about the old one. There are several ways this can happen, and they aren't mutually exclusive.

Relief. You fall in love too fast, just to get relief from the pain; but your heart isn't free, isn't available yet, so the next person gets a bum deal.

Revenge. "I'll show him," you say about your ex. "He thinks I'm lovelorn and bereft; okay, I'll get involved with a *great guy* and see how he likes *that!*"

So the fuel that drives the locomotive of love is not interest in the new person, but desire to show up the old one. Too bad for the great guy.

Any Port in a Storm. You choose a *totally inappropriate* object, just to have love happening again. You get it on with the next interested guy who appears, even though you have nothing in common with him and don't even like the way he kisses.

Hasty Diagnosis. You misidentify the factors that made the last relationship sicken and die, and armed with that false vaccine, you set out to avoid the same infection in the future—and you walk right into it.

We have already looked at two forms of this mistake. One was the wounded ego's message, "You loved and look what it did: it got you hurt and got me insulted. The pathogen was love. So let's avoid that." The result is future relationships ruined by being too well defended—a state of permanent rebound.

Case two was the victim of cheating. Because dishonesty and leaving characterized the last guy, she sets out to find someone who is wearing a sign saying "Honest" or a sign saying "Won't leave". Or she fixates on accidental features of the ex, and looks for their opposites in the next dude.

Flight from the Truth. The new relationship is used as a way of running from, hiding from, the implications of the old one. A way to avoid realizing what just happened to you.

Now we're at the crux of the matter. You take one glance at the past and it's too scary. The truth about what went wrong is complicated and facing it would involve really looking at the problems of you and him—and worse than that, of *love*. That's right, we want to hang on to our romantic ideals, our fairy-tale illusions; so we tell ourselves "that wasn't love; it doesn't count. But this new one will be."

So we plunge into a new relationship, not because we are paying attention to the past, but to *avoid* listening to it. We use the new relationship as a distraction. But that just means we won't be able to honor it.

The new, "rebound" relationship gets short shrift. It is rendered unreal by the feared, hated, misperceived reality of the old relationship. Your past is trying to tell you something. But you're not listening. It's like a face at your window, seen in the night, and you ran from it and hid in the closet, when it was really a neighbor trying to tell you that a fire was coming.

Playing the Blame Game Badly. When we can't deal with the real story, we oversimplify it. This is never more true than when it's time to hand out blame. It's much easier to say "It was all his fault" or "It was all my fault" than to say, "okay, we each screwed up in various ways, and we even screwed up as a team."

But blaming your partner for everything is rebound logic. It exaggerates the destructive power of the other gender.

cole and billie

Cole was a tall, lean drink of water, forty-five years old, who wore snakeskin boots and had an aquiline face and thinning rusty hair that he defiantly wore long. He was a bohemian kind of guy who made his living as a free-lance photographer, mostly in the music business. He met Billie in a Denny's restaurant at three in the morning. She was sitting in the next booth, reading a book. She looked to be late thirties, had thick toffee-colored hair and cleavage.

Cole noticed that she was reading a beat-up paperback of *The Sun Also Rises*.

At one point she looked up at him and smiled.

"Good book?" he said, just to test her. He had his own copy at home.

"I used to think so," she said.

Cole laughed. He had reread the novel a couple years ago and found it mystifying. Men sauntered from one Parisian café to another, engaging in banter that couldn't ever have been witty, and obsessing on a woman who appeared to be completely shallow. He had decided that he had outgrown Hemingway. There was a degree of tough that merged into stupidity.

She moved into his booth and he spiked her coffee too.

Cole poured a little Jack from his metal flask into his coffee.

"That looks like fun," Billie said.

She moved into his booth and he spiked her coffee too, and they started talking. Turned out she lived south of Nashville and was managing a new singer on the way up. Who needed photographs.

Cole had been single for a few years, after a bitter divorce. Though he was in no hurry to get involved again, he was very attracted to Billie. They had a lot in common: they'd both lived in Bakersfield in their younger days, were both well read, and were both mavericks still trying to do some good work in a country music scene gone shallow.

They walked out to Billie's pickup. Cole was in no hurry, but he sensed something volatile in her, something that moved him. He wanted to taste her lips. He did and they both got lost in it, like a drug.

Several kisses later she stopped and held him at arm's length. "I should warn you," she said, "I'm just getting over someone. I've kind of lost my nerve."

This was just the wrong thing to say, if she wanted to discourage him, because Cole had a deep vein of the rescuer in him. She made him promise he wouldn't hurt her, and he said of course not. He loved the idea of having to go slow and gentle and kind. It fit perfectly with his own hard-earned caution.

In spite of their best intentions, these two found their way to bed five times in the next two weeks. Mostly they ended up at Cole's place, because it was in town and he lived alone. One time he went to her farm in Franklin and he met the young singer she was working with, Skye, who was staying there. Skye was a sexy, slim brunette of about twenty-three with an older woman's voice. She was full of spit and vinegar, and excited that Cole was going to take photos of her. She flirted with him but this was only entertainment in his eyes; she reminded him of his daughter. He also met a friend of Billie's, a songwriter named Robert who was her quasi-business partner.

It wasn't about sex for Cole, though the sex was wonderful. He had already admitted to himself that he was in love with Billie; he had already decided that this was for keeps. Billie didn't want to talk about her ex yet, but Skye told Cole a little about him. "They were supposed to get engaged, but he chickened out," she said. "Really hurt Billie. She'll need time to believe in someone again." Once more, patience was called for—and Cole was ready and willing.

Billie created an impossible job description for the next guy.

Then one night Cole was assigned to cover a live recording at a legendary venue. The place was full of the famous and the would-be-famous. All the tables were pushed together in a circle around the performers, and Cole's reserved seat was at one end of a table of people he didn't know. He didn't have to snap pictures till the second set, so for now he could relax. The table next to him filled up and one of the last to sit down was his new acquaintance Skye, right beside him. They chatted a bit before the show, then Skye whispered things like "awesome" in his ear a couple of times during the performance.

The rest of the night Cole was pretty busy covering the event, but he did run into Billie's friend Robert in the hall outside the bathroom, and Robert seemed very sarcastic.

After the show Cole stayed in the bar, hanging out with the owner and some other old friends long after it closed. An hour before dawn he drove home. He was surprised to find Billie waiting for him, *inside* his apartment.

"How did you get in here?" he asked, pleased yet somehow uneasy.

"That doesn't matter," she said.

"You just had to do it, didn't you?" she said.

"I'm sorry?"

"I heard about you and Skye. I've already taken care of her."

Billie then pointed a gun at Cole. Tears came out of her eyes but her aim was steady. "You know that my last boyfriend dumped me for a younger woman," she said.

"No, I didn't know that," Cole said, inching towards her.

"Robert told me you met Skye at the club," Billie said. "He saw you coming on to her."

"That's silly," Cole said. "I didn't even know she was going to be there."

"This ends now," Billie said, and she pulled the trigger.

Okay, that surprised me a little bit too.

I'm guessing you and I are not going to reach for a gun in this situation, but we may easily follow the same logic, and the sheer naked simplicity of Billie's response makes it easier to appreciate what that cracked logic is.

Billie wasn't really seeing the new man who was standing in front of her. She was projecting onto him her livid image of the previous guy. And what she was trying to end, was a sequence of events from the past. It should have been over, but she was keeping it alive by replaying it in her mind.

Not accurately though, because Billie had distorted that past. Contrary to the story she had created and internalized, her ex had in fact been a fairly nice guy, who sensed that he was wrong for her and withdrew in a timely fashion. (He then met another woman who was more his speed. Yes, she was younger, but he met her *after* leaving Billie.)

Billie, too overwrought to assess blame fairly, had essentially demonized her ex. By thus exaggerating his power over her, Billie created an impossible job description for the next guy. He had to be utterly without claws, a dude who would be totally manageable (with the likely result that she would tire of him)—or else, if he had any red blood in him, she would turn him into a repeat of the devil she saw in the old guy. Either way it wouldn't work out.

With the echo of Billie's shot in our heads, we may be able to appreciate the incredible warped power of the rebounding brain.

Being on the rebound is getting a superficial take on the failed relationship and running with that, instead of drilling down to the truth. That cuts off our ability to be in the present. Without knowing it, we carry onward a template of the past, and everything that happens is distorted by that filter, which is itself a distortion of what really happened. Because we've avoided really examining the failed relationship, our twisted version of it slips into place as the lens through which we see everything. So we aren't really *in* the new moment, we aren't really *with* the new person. Instead we're in an endless dysfunctional triangle consisting of ourself, the new person, and the maligned ghost of our ex.

I think it's pretty clear that we want to avoid that. When we find a new person, we want to be fully with them, true to the new possibilities. In choosing them and in interacting with them, we want to *benefit* from our past experience, not be roughed up by it. That requires calmly examining it. So let's go that way.

12

what went wrong

the two scenarios

*W*hen two people fail, there are *reasons*. It isn't just the fickle winds blowing.

Sometimes these reasons are obvious and even laughable, and any lessons are learned by sun-up. Sometimes the only message you need to pick up is, "He was a loser. Move on."

But I'll be talking about more serious relationships here, where you made a real try, took risks, thought you had it right, and were adversely affected by the outcome. These relationships need to be listened to; they hold the keys to your future. Because, as I said earlier, those who don't study history are condemned to repeat it.

Failed relationships contain a map that can lead you to successful love; but that map is written in code and it has to be deciphered. When you understand what went wrong, and what went right, what worked for you, what you liked and what you didn't, it is as if a blank sheet develops into a photograph, a picture of your future.

Doing the work of delving into the past is empowering. It makes you feel as if you can understand this stuff—it doesn't have to be a jumble of confusing emotions. Once you sort things out, you realize that you can do better next time; you have choices and you can make them in a more informed way. The challenge of choosing a good mate and having a good relationship doesn't have to be an inscrutable mystery; it is something you can apply your intelligence to.

HOW TO STRUCTURE OUR PROBE OF THE PAST

When we look at our failed relationships, most of the time we tend to go one of two ways. Either we say, "That never really had a chance; even though we tried, we were just wrong for each other." Or we say, "You know, we were a pretty good match. We could have been soulmates, maybe we were. But somehow, we blew it."

Behind these two ways of evaluating the past, lies the concept of compatibility. The first scenario says you weren't really compatible with your partner; the second that you were. Because I think compatibility is so important to love's chances, I'm going to use it as a way of structuring our review. Now I think we often have a gut sense of which scenario we were in. But I will offer some clues that can help you decide. The dividing line between the two scenarios is not always a hard-and-fast one: some failed relationships may partake of both. What is important is that if you examine your past relationship in terms of these two scenarios, you will ask the right questions and learn the right lessons about it. So I will devote five chapters to the first scenario, and two longer chapters to the second. Here's a preview.

scenario a: you were a bad match for each other

The reason that many relationships fail is that people are with the wrong people. They choose someone who isn't right for them and then spend years trying to make it work, but in the end it doesn't. Even then, it can be hard to see that you were simply in a mismatch. The next two chapters will present clues that can indicate you were in this situation. The past starts talking to you as soon as the breakup has happened, and sometimes its way of telling you that you were with the wrong person is that you experience an upswing.

A blank sheet develops into a photograph, a picture of your future.

After we look at that unexpected good news, and its messages for the future, I'll move to the next piece of the Scenario A puzzle: how to unlock the "guide to incompatibility" that is written in your own history. Not only will this discussion free you from a bunch of false lessons that a mismatch tries to foist on you, but it will yield up a whole inventory of things that you'll want to look for in your next partner, the lack of which made your ex a bad match for you. To complete our investigation of Scenario A, I will turn to a fascinating topic: how do we end up with the wrong person; why does this happen so often? This will lead us to some important questions: what is "falling in love," can it be relied on, and do we sometimes misuse it?

scenario b: you were basically a good match for each other

You *weren't* wrong for each other; it should have worked out between you, but it didn't. This is a story line that can haunt you for a long time, the story of what might have been. And it also has direct implications for your next relationship. That's because next time around you are hopefully going to choose someone with whom you are hugely compatible, so you'll be faced with exactly the same challenge that Scenario B says you were faced with last time. But you'll want to achieve a different result. So I will spend two chapters focusing on the ways that a good match may have gone wrong, and what needs to be done next time, so it will go right.

We begin with Scenario A: you and your partner were not a good match.

13

the unexpected upturn

the first clue that you were with the wrong person

In Part One of this book we toured a battlefield, after the battle was over. We assessed damage, examined wounds, started treatments. But in that aftermath of a relationship, something else is sometimes found. There can be green shoots growing out of the charred ground. Signs of renewal and revival. These are the first whispers of the past talking to you, beginning to give you the lowdown on the mismatch that was.

the return of kate

After Kate and Ben split up, Kate's long-time friend Sarah took a lot of calls from Kate. Ben had moved back to Arizona and Kate would

This wasn't the drooping Kate that she had seen for the past two years, the Kate that was part of "Kate & Ben."

always cry on the phone, saying it should have worked out and what had she done wrong and how much she missed Ben. Sarah had never really thought Ben was the right guy for Kate and couldn't imagine missing him. But Kate sounded just awful.

Then one night Sarah went to a gallery opening, a new show for some local artists that she'd read about in the free weekly. A mere month had gone by since the breakup, during which the two friends had not seen each other in person.

Sarah was munching a tasty Huevos Roll when Kate first appeared. Sarah was flabbergasted. This wasn't the drooping Kate that she had seen for the past two years, the Kate that was part of "Kate & Ben."

This was the Kate that God had made. She glowed like a light bulb, shed energy into the room. She had lost weight. Her hair was back to its natural color, an odd shade of very pale blond that just happened to accentuate her topaz blue eyes.

"You look amazing," Sarah said.

"I guess I'm doing alright," Kate said. "Trying to soldier on."

The two women toured the show. There were some cool black-and-white photos of people in a zoo. There were wall hangings made of hemp and painted wood. Then they got to some watercolor paintings showing the world seen through the windshield of a car. The driver's point of view. There was a shabby man in the rain, crossing right in front of the car. A movie marquee at dawn. A couple arm in arm on a dirt road. They were dazzling, full of the motion of the car, glimpses of other lives.

Sarah said, "I love these."

Kate said, "Thank you."

Sarah hadn't even known Kate was in the show. It seemed Kate had been working on this series for a while, but since Ben was gone she had nothing else to do so she really got into it and finished them. She hadn't shown any new work for over a year, and here she was, back with a vengeance.

"How did you do these?" Sarah asked her.

"I took digital photos while driving, just snapped them. Then I worked them up into paintings."

"I can't believe you." Sarah hugged Kate, squeezed her with delight. They had some wine and Sarah said, "You realize what is going on, don't you?"

It took a while for Kate to admit it. But then she was able to articulate the truth. Thinking back, she realized that almost from the day Ben had left, certain things had been happening to her. And every one of them told her she was better off without Ben.

- *She started to think more clearly.* How could this be? Well, in his spare hours Ben liked to create a haze of beer and dope and food and if Kate wanted to be with him, that was where he could be joined, so she went there too. Ben had different values than Kate. Ben worshipped celebrity and success as shown on TV and tended to like whatever had the highest ratings. Kate was brought down by TV; it sabotaged her faith in original, authentic thought because there was so little of that to be found on it. In a strange way, Ben confused Kate's mind. He didn't mean to, but he was so rigid in his thinking, so black-and-white about everything, that it weakened Kate's grip on the gray areas of life that interested her most, the subtle gradations where her truth was found.

> Maybe it comes down to how much affection you have for reality. Ben didn't have much.

- *She remembered which things mattered to her.* It's hard to hang on to your implausible dream when people around you are just going for the obvious, just taking the well-trodden paths. Sometimes you need some clear air so your own goals can be seen in the distance. Ben was a very talented painter, as a technician; in fact, it had been he who had once helped Kate make her breakthrough with watercolors. But he didn't do any painting anymore. That path had just petered out, in favor of a courier gig and a couch potato avocation. When the distractions and misdirections of Ben were removed, Kate remembered that what she chiefly wanted was to pursue her art.

- *She shook herself and said, "I can't stand to be this unhealthy."* Kate was not naturally an abuser of alcohol and drugs. Ben was. She was a party animal and a rowdy soul, but she didn't need a lot of artificial help. Maybe it comes down to how much affection you have for reality. Ben didn't have much. He was happiest when the room was a little hazy and he could lose himself. The movie or the football game or the reality show was the whole universe and he didn't exist, except as part of it. Kate wanted to exist. Kate wanted to be awake. Without Ben around she naturally began running again, and started to shop for healthy food. She drank less and smoked a *lot* less, because such moderation was no longer considered anti-social in her home.

- *She started looking like herself.* If a woman is her own artistic creation, Kate's had become a little distorted. As we have seen, she had a natural shade of ash blond that seemed to have been cleverly designed to complement her pale skin and unearthly blue eyes. Changing that hair to a yellower hue had been Ben's idea, and it had ruined the effect. He liked more make-up too, on a person who needed little, and he wanted girlier get-ups that made Kate just a little phony. All of this was shed as effortlessly as the color that soon washed out of Kate's hair.

- *She was funny again.* Kate had a fearless quality to her sense of humor. Some of her best stuff was when she skewered her friends' small hypocrisies, mercilessly pointing out when they were trying to sweep inconvenient truths under the rug or put a dignified spin on things. This edge had gotten a little dull, maybe because her life with Ben was supported by too many rationalizations that didn't bear scrutiny. Now that she was free to live authentically, she started scoring the big laughs again.

- *She started feeling sexy.* Each of us has our own sexual agenda, and if we can't find a way to mesh that with our partner's, it atrophies. When the partner is gone our truest hankerings resurface. Ben had lost interest in Kate sexually after about four months of novelty, and that had made her feel unattractive and unsensual. She was a very sexual being, so this meant a serious loss. Now she remembered who she was and how much pleasure she could give and receive. She had actually wondered if she was losing her libido. No—the sap of desire was running again.

- *She felt free.* Freedom is a strange thing. We think of it in grand terms—the ability to hit the road and drive all night to anywhere—but even in a domestic form it can be intensely sweet. Kate found herself savoring small liberties, like:

  · She could eat whatever she wanted, whenever she wanted. When Ben was around she had tried to tug food towards regular meals that at least bordered on being healthy, and she didn't snack even when she wanted to, because that would always cause him to do the same. Now she was alone and she took delight in following her own impulses, which led to such scandalous things as blueberries, almonds, and oat bran cereal.

  · She could read while eating, because Ben wasn't there to interrupt her or put the TV on.

· She could wear exactly what she wanted, including nothing. When Ben had been there, she of course was affected by his tastes (though he had never let her cramp his lack of style). When she wore sweatpants and a T-shirt, she felt sloppy. Now she could just not worry about it; but surprisingly, she found herself sometimes wearing gorgeous things just for the fun of it. She started enjoying clothes, and her own style, again.

· She could put music on while puttering around the house. This had been a problem with Ben, because he didn't like the same acoustic stuff she did, and because that pesky TV was usually on if he was around—and he was *always* around. Kate now discovered some of the cool music channels that came with her cable TV—like bluegrass and girl folk—and suddenly was exploring new music again.

These and other recoveries that Kate experienced were signs that during the relationship with Ben she had suffered *loss of identity*. What Sarah saw was an almost surreal change, as if a disguise had been removed and the real Kate had appeared. Soon, Kate was firing on all cylinders.

If you find that after a breakup your own identity seems to be returning with a vengeance, that is a strong indicator that you and your partner were not a good match. You may still believe that he had worth. You may still miss him, and you may be sad some of the time, but that doesn't mean you should neglect the signals that your own nature is sending your way.

By paying attention to the resurgence of your own identity, by tallying the ways in which your real self is returning, you'll be unlocking the lessons of the past. Your own multi-faceted recovery tells you that you and your ex were a bad match in a number of very specific ways. As we saw in Kate's story, the ways in which another person undermines your identity are not always that easy to detect while they're happening, but they can be very clear in retrospect. So take careful note of them, because we all have a tendency to repeat the same patterns, and these may be your own special pitfalls. Guard against them in the future and, on the positive side, remember that you can get a good reading on a new person by being aware of which facets of you flourish in his presence.

It is very easy for one's true self to be swamped, eclipsed, or repressed in the throes of a bad relationship. In trying to edit yourself to someone else's specifications, you can lose touch with who you really are. When that ends, you make friends with yourself again.

And not just yourself . . .

14

love me, love my friends

_A_nother clue to whether or not your past relationship was with Mr. Right or Mr. Wrong comes in the form of a very particular sensation— that of a wall dissolving around you. Sometimes the dissolution of a couple feels like an end to isolation. It's as if the merger of you and your partner somehow made a barrier around you that kept other souls at a distance.

Then that wall is gone and you find yourself calling people that you haven't kept up with: your mother, your brother, your friends. You don't feel cut off from them anymore; you're able to pick up the thread where it was dropped.

After a while, you didn't see very much of the people he was resistant to.

The story you have to tell them is no longer out of tune. Somehow when you were with your partner, you couldn't report freely about your life to the people who matter most to you. Conversations became superficial, degenerated into small talk. You could only tell them part of the truth, and that wasn't enough to strike sparks across a distance. Maybe you weren't telling _yourself_ the whole truth, so it was hard to talk to people with whom you are naturally honest.

Again, this resurgence is a message about the relationship that ended. It is telling you that your ex was a bad match for you. In his presence, your connections with others tended to wilt.

the subversive partner

The decline may have been fairly mild, as in the previous example where connections were still there but they felt more tenuous; or it could have been a precipitous drop. That happened if your partner actively opposed your outside relationships, or put up roadblocks to them. He may have done this by playing any of several roles:

> *The Loyalty Enforcer.* Your partner treated you as if you were being unfaithful to him, when you tried to spend time alone with other people. This possessiveness masquerading as suspicion is a sticky snare. It is very easy to start feeling guilty about innocent behavior when your partner doesn't trust you, and then you may start to *act* guilty and you are really trapped. The real impetus behind this treatment is more likely that your partner wasn't confident that what he had to offer you was enough, and he worried that by bonding with others you would realize his shortcomings.

The tipping point came when Martin started trying to take Nancy's place in her own family.

> *The Non-participant.* When you asked your partner to go with you to occasions that would naturally demand a couple, he begged off *if certain people were involved.* Which discouraged you enough that you didn't go either. Or you went alone and then he resented that, so you didn't go the next time. After a while,

you didn't see very much of the people he was resistant to. Without declaring himself openly, just by reluctance and foot-dragging he managed to limit your social sphere to the parts that he was comfortable with.

This can be a very insidious form of selection. It's as if your partner is driving past various nightclubs that are your social life, and is deciding which of them the two of you shall not patronize. Wouldn't it be unfortunate if his insecurity made him avoid the ones which are most colorful, challenging, and otherwise valuable?

The Critic. A more direct approach is to critique your friends. Your partner cleverly analyzed their faults and shortcomings, so that now you had to either abandon them or refute him. This could have been a sincere thing, caused by his misperceiving them. He thought friend A was obnoxious when what she was, was irreverent. He thought friend B was snotty when what she was, was smart. He thought friend C was boring when what she was, was shy (around him). Or he found one of your friends to be an evil schemer, and he taught you that your affection had been naïve, when the truth was your friend had been looking out for you.

If your partner was sincere, then at least he had the defence of honesty; but one has to question whether he was the right guy for you. If he *wasn't* sincere and was really just manipulating you out of possessiveness or paranoia, that is an even better ground for finding him unworthy. So when someone becomes the arbiter of your friends, that's a huge red flag—and will be in future.

The Thief of Hearts. You may have run across an even more extreme and somewhat bizarre way of undermining your existing relationships—competing for your friends.

Martin was one of these collectors of souls. He saw people as a sort of commodity, and his goal was to have more in his portfolio than others did. Online, he was obsessed with recruiting "friends" to his myspace list, and he constantly checked others' lists to make sure they had fewer than he did. His approach to the real world was not different.

After he'd been dating Nancy for a while, Martin began to make private forays into her large, vibrant circle of friends. He would go on his own to visit couples she knew, hang out with them for an evening and pour on the charm. Nancy would sometimes hear from them that he had been around, and would feel just a little strange about it. And Martin would mention to her that he had been talking to so-and-so, in a kind of boastful way, as if she should know he was outdoing her. Then she started noticing that some of her friends weren't as warm to her as they had been—they seemed a little awkward. The tipping point came when Martin started trying to take Nancy's place in her own family of origin. That got quashed fast, from both sides.

After she and Martin broke up, his bonds with her circle crumbled, and as she got close to those people again, the truth emerged. Martin had been making alliances with them, as if he was an enemy nation conspiring against Nancy. He had been subtly bad-mouthing her to her own friends, to try to reduce her stock of people while increasing his.

If, in examining your own past relationship, you find that any of these maneuvers were afoot, you have had a major insight into what went wrong. A partner who reacted that way to your friendships was not the right partner for you. Although this kind of negative campaign can be subtle at the time, it often becomes blatantly clear after the breakup, when your friendships return to form. And it's easier to detect the next time around.

In the following story I will look at a couple who in fact had the goods in this area. But at one point there was a misstep that caused serious hurt, and it will take us to the very positive core of the matter.

the sacred link: why ellen cried

Ron and Ellen were a fortyish couple living in Bloomington, Indiana, and nicely embarked on what shaped up to be a long and rich relationship. It was their first Christmas together and they were visiting Ellen's parents in Willow Grove near Philadelphia. Ron was a bit overwhelmed by the onslaught of Ellen's tribe: the parents, three siblings, their little kids, and assorted friends old and young dropping in every day. He liked them pretty well and was especially partial to Ellen's mom and to one of her brothers, but he was a bit shy and preferred to take his time in getting to know people. He could only take so much exposure to a noisy, churning group before he either felt invisible or felt he was getting the third degree. Ellen's family were especially daunting because they specialized in a rapid-fire, rapier wit, and at the first major sit-down dinner Ron felt like he was ducking under sniper fire. Their perfect ease with each others' humor made him feel like an outsider.

> Through bleary eyes Ron saw that she was already washed and dried and putting a nice blouse on over a black bra.

Nevertheless Ron really liked Ellen, and wanted to become comfortable with her family, because she was very close to them and she seemed so proud to present him. So he tried, really tried to engage and to find the right compromise between coming on too strong and not coming on at all. He reminded himself that the trick is to listen, and that it wasn't about him, and he did okay.

But by the day after Christmas, Ron had just about exhausted his store of energy and patience. He wanted to be back in Bloomington in a house with two people in it. He was a bit testy at bedtime as they crawled into the lumpy twin beds in what had once been the kids' room, and when Ellen reminded him that the next morning she wanted him to go with her to have breakfast with someone named Maria, he just grunted and buried his face in the pillow. Ellen had told him about a lot of friends, and he didn't really remember which one this was—they were a blur in his mind.

So morning came and Ron found Ellen shaking his shoulder. He had had a restless night but had finally reached an uneasy détente with the bed and was sunk in the kind of sleep that wants three or four more hours. "Last call for the shower," Ellen said in a voice whose playfulness was a tad brittle.

Through bleary eyes Ron saw that she was already washed and dried and putting a nice blouse on over a black bra. Somehow the sight of her looking so fetching made him more irritated. He said, "Look, you go. I am exhausted."

"But I want you to meet Maria."

"I'll meet her another time." He rolled over facing the wall and hoped for the sound of an exit. What he heard was silence, then sniffing.

He twisted and found his beautiful woman crying, looking at him with anger and hurt in her big brown eyes; but he just didn't get it and he turned away again.

"I don't appreciate this," she said, and she left.

Later that day Ellen returned, her eyes bright and her cheeks ruddy from the winter day, and she told Ron all about her breakfast with Maria and it dawned on Ron that of all the people Ellen had told him about, this was the one he would most like to have met. Maria was a dear friend with whom Ellen had once worked, a talented person who shared some major interests with Ron (including his obsession with the civil war), and according to Ellen, Maria had the best eyes on the planet, deep and knowing and generous.

Ron had had a useless morning, had never gotten back to sleep, and had arisen to an empty house where he couldn't seem to muster any breakfast—so he had lost out on every count.

In spite of this little setback, Ellen and Ron made a go of their relationship, and he became very close with her family, once he got over being intimidated. Ellen often teased him about that lazy morning when he failed to meet the marvelous Maria. Meanwhile Ron's friends in Bloomington took to Ellen in a big way, and he found more sap coursing through his own social tree than had been true for a long time. He had been in danger of becoming a hermit before he met Ellen, and a hermit wasn't the real him.

We take the measure of our partners when we expose them to the people we cherish.

Then, three years after that first Christmas, Ron met Maria when she came to Bloomington to visit. She was even more illustrious than he had been led to believe. She interviewed him in a bold way that made him feel revealed and honored, and then, to Ellen's delight, he did the same back. The three of them cooked and they talked and they played scrabble and they laughed and cried and didn't get to bed till the wee hours.

And after she was gone Ron and Ellen talked, and they figured out why Ellen had cried on that December morning. This is what they worked out:

> Part of the sacred bond between two people is that each one trusts the other to know them well enough to know which people they need to meet and might really like. The

desire to share one's most valued friends with one's mate is itself a form of trust, a belief in the mate's worthiness. It was that trust that Ron had violated (or failed to muster) the morning he didn't get up with Ellen to go have breakfast with Maria. *And that's why Ellen cried:* he was showing lack of faith in her knowledge of him, and lack of gratitude for her wanting to give him a valued gift.

Putting it another way: we take the measure of our partners when we expose them to the people we cherish. They test us and we test them when they meet our loved ones. Ellen cried because Ron was ducking the true test. And the true opportunity.

A new couple calls on faith.

Look back at the relationship that ended. Take careful stock of how it affected your most valued connections with other people. When those special tests (or opportunities) arose, what happened? If your findings are negative, you have learned an important lesson about what went wrong.

And what to look for next time. To paraphrase the poet, no person is an island. We are each partially *constituted* by our bonds with the family members and friends we love most. If a man really wants to know you, he wants to know the people you love.

So look for these signs. A good partner will be a shrewd observer of your interactions with your friends. He will be highly entertained by watching your antics with them, and will revel in the knowledge of you that can be gained that way. A good partner will enrich your best relationships.

In a healthy couple, your circle of friends won't contract; it will expand.

We've taken a look at two kinds of upswing that can signal, after a relationship is over, that you were with the wrong person. I've called that situation Scenario A: where you and your partner were basically incompatible. It's time now to take a more comprehensive look at incompatibility, and the false and true lessons it holds.

15

the wrong partner

how you wrote your own personal guide to incompatibility

$\mathcal{T}$he good news is, while spending those months or years with the partner who just wasn't right for you, you were conducting your own clinic on compatibility. No one else can tell you who you are compatible with, and it's sometimes hard to figure out in the abstract; but when you're actually *with* someone, all the cogs and gears get tested. When you're with someone who is wrong for you, you find out a *lot*. You learn which parts of couple interaction matter most to you, and you learn what you need a partner to bring to the table.

Incompatibility, if not understood, reads as personal inadequacy.

A WORKSHOP ON COMPATIBILITY

The devil is in the details, and I have a feeling that's where the angels are too.

So it's time to marshal your intuition and your memory, and those thoughts that you haven't had time to unfold, and make an unflinching assessment of the relationship that didn't last.

As we move through our workshop on compatibility, ponder how you and your ex fared in its various departments, how significant they were in the failure of the relationship, and how important they are to you now, through eyes that are wiser. In the light of a failed relationship, you may find that your needs and wants have emerged and evolved—have crystallized into a pretty clear portrait of the kind of man who would be a better match for you, the next time around.

Compatibility doesn't mean being the *same* as your partner. It means fitting together well with him. In some areas, people can thrive on not being similar: for example, body type and life skills. But in other areas, such as values, intellect, and sexual agenda, they may be better off if they're more alike. As I present different facets of human beings, take your own reading on the past and what you want to look for in the future.

If sex is half of compatibility, then friendship is the other ninety percent.

Please don't get the impression that I'm saying compatibility is a multiple choice type of affair, where you can just check off a bunch of boxes. You *can* get a "long shot" of a person that tells you in a general way if he is in your ball park (this is particularly easy to do online, before you even look at profiles), but real compatibility waits in the close-up of time you spend together. It resides in the *details* of how two people get along, the texture of their rapport: how they communicate, how they have fun, what they share, what they admire in each other, how they work as a team. And your past relationship has much to tell you about that.

But such tips are only half the reason for this exercise. There's another, equally important benefit, which will open up a whole new vista of healing. It can be put as follows: **Incompatibility, if not understood, reads as personal inadequacy.**

When you emerge from a mismatched relationship, there is a tendency to internalize every failure, to come away with a sad list of the new "facts" you've learned about yourself. *I'm not an interesting person; I'm a complainer; I'm a bore; I'm gutless; I'm bad in bed . . .* The logic here is: I wasn't good for that person, so I must not be good for *any*one.

That's the typical damage that ensues from a mismatch that *hasn't yet been understood.* Which is why discovering that you were incompatible with someone is liberation. It's a priceless step forward. Until you figure it out, you can't help blaming your own flaws (or your partner's) for the many slip-ups that were made. But once you get it, you can begin to put away the pointer of blame. In so many instances, nothing was wrong with you (or him); it was the *combination* of you and him that was wrong. Not only blame but anger and guilt begin to melt away.

The next step is to heal the feeling of inadequacy. The goal is to exonerate yourself, and eventually to re-validate yourself, in every area where a mismatched relationship has left you feeling like a loser. As I go through the different areas, I will mention examples of false take-aways—mistaking incompatibility for inadequacy—that should be rejected because they are not true and they are not worthy of the person you are.

friendship

Someone once said, if sex is half of compatibility, then friendship is the other ninety percent.

So the most general question is this: Were you and your partner really simpatico? Or to put it a different way, would you have wanted him as a friend if you hadn't had a sexual thing going? If your response is no, then ask yourself: in what areas did you need more in common, in order that the answer might have been yes?

Those are areas that need to click with your next partner. As we get down to specifics, many possible answers will emerge.

A false take-away
My expectations of enjoying time alone with my partner were just too high.

personality and emotional makeup

There are many ways in which two personalities can fail to mesh. Here are some examples to look for.

the feisty quotient

Some people are born to fight. They like to argue; they like dissention in the air; it gets their blood flowing; maybe it spells home because that was how it was in the house they grew up in. Others find combat draining and discouraging. Looking back, were you and your ex in different camps? A person who is averse to the feeling of hostility is more likely to want to patch things up quickly and without damage; so it's better if she is with someone who shares that preference. On the other hand, bickering can be a fine pastime for those who enjoy it.

Of course, there are going to be some unavoidable issues and disagreements. But fighters are going to handle them differently than peacemakers. Where did you find yourself on this spectrum?

A false take-away
I'm a pushover; I'll have to change before I can be in an equal relationship. Or: I'm way too feisty. I'll have to tone that down if I want a good match.

gender and polarity

Traditional stereotypes of masculinity and femininity still hang like ancient moons in our cultural sky, but meanwhile down here on the earth, things are not so hidebound. For example, manliness is associated with physical bravery and fighting spirit; and women are said to excel at emotional communication and nurturing. But are the virtues of the two genders always that different? Your average female trial attorney doesn't give way to any man for coolness in combat; women face the rigors of childbirth that make men cower. Many men are excellent communicators about feelings, and lots of guys are good or even great at nurturing.

Still there is this delicious polarity that we relish, and it lends heat to sexual goings-on. For many of us, certain members of the opposite sex have an overall aura, strongly related to their physical characteristics but also to their mind, that moves us. "Man," a certain guy's vibe says to a certain woman, and her being says "woman" to him. This is very subjective stuff. A guy who seems like a sheep to one woman may seem like a wolf to another; and a woman whose presence screams *female* to one guy may not arouse any great gender turbulence in another. A certain shape, a certain face, a certain walk—the right kind of hair, the right voice, the right smile, can all figure in. We may not be able to define it, but we sure know it when we see it.

What often happens in successful couples is that there's a sort of envelope that strikes the other person as simple and relatable: *I am man to you and you are woman to me.* Then within each person there may be ingredients that test the old stereotypes, but these complications only seem to juice the fun. I talked to one couple who had polarity in spades. They were like opposite magnets: when they stood together he seemed the definition of man and she of woman. Yet when they started telling their story, it was full of blown stereotypes. She was a tough administrator and he a pushover with his staff; she was thick-skinned while he was sensitive and easily hurt. The list went on. They were both completely comfortable with these quirks and were hilarious while talking about them.

And maybe that's the most important thing. Not how feminine or masculine a person is in some conventional sense, but have they found a partner with whom their own unique flavor works?

Some people subscribe to a more traditional version of masculine and feminine, and some don't. This is fine if you're with someone whose code matches yours. The thing to beware of is a person who tries, in a dogmatic way, to enforce a rigid notion of how each gender should be, where this rigidity is actually a disguised insecurity, a fear of the variations that exist within oneself.

When thinking about your last partner, ask yourself:

- Was there a problem because the two of you had different ideas about what it means for a man to be masculine, or for a woman to be feminine, or about *how* masculine or feminine one should be?

- Did you have the overall sense of polarity that you would want?

- Did being with your partner make you feel easy about your own unique mix of qualities, so you could celebrate being a human and not a stereotype?

A false take-away
It has now been proven: I am not feminine enough.

insecurities and complaints
Did one of you like to vent fear and annoyance, as a way of coping, and did the other find that a nuisance? Better to find someone who likes your approach to life's terrors and its adversity.

A false take-away
I'm just a big complainer.

intelligence/intellect/words

There are different kinds of intelligence. Someone who is not book-smart may build a business empire. It is unfair to expect your partner to be brilliant in exactly the ways that you are. In fact it is beneficial to a couple if they bring different talents to the table, because more challenges can be met and there can be a division of labor.

But still . . . but still. In core areas of your mentality, you need to be able to reach your spouse. You need not just good, but great communication. It's up to you to decide what these core areas are, and your past relationship can help you. Were there topics that were too important to neglect, and yet you and he couldn't get it on? The things you care about, you need to share. Some of them can only be shared in words.

Someone who is not book-smart may build a business empire.

Here are a couple of bare minimums, bars you *had* to be able to get over. If you couldn't, it speaks volumes about the one you'll need next time.

- You got home from work and you wanted to tell your mate a delicious story that happened that day, a story that involved a couple of technicalities about your job. You tried to tell him but he couldn't grasp the technicalities, even though you explained them clearly. So the story died.

- You had a problem with a friend. You were all broken up about it, because you loved this person and things were going wrong. You tried to get your spouse's counsel. The conversation went nowhere.

- You and your mate had a peak experience. You wanted to talk about it, because you like to analyze things that move you deeply. He didn't, so he wouldn't.

Any of these scenarios could be reversed; it could be that he wanted to talk about things that you couldn't get into. There is no fault here. There is just a pair of people who don't fit.

A false take-away
I am an effete, eggheaded over-analyzer of everything, who doesn't deserve to live. Oh, and way too verbal.

abuse

It may seem ridiculous to list abuse as a type of incompatibility—it's like saying a tornado is a kind of thunderstorm.

But in fact there are different kinds of abuse and one of them springs directly from incompatibility. The other kind is more dire but it signals a mismatch too, the kind where a person is no good for *any*one, not just for you—which is the most extreme case of incompatibility. Let me take them in order.

when one partner doesn't fit the other's requirements

If partner A doesn't appeal to partner B's tastes, A will automatically end up in a state much like being abused, even if B isn't a particularly bad person. In the end, even if they try, people can't hide the truth about what pleases them and displeases them. A person who doesn't like you the way you naturally are is the perfect person to make you feel bad about yourself. Their mere presence is a form of ill-treatment.

> Unsolicited admiration is a very nice ally to self-esteem.

Let's take body type as an example. Some men have a marked preference for a thin woman. Whether this is hard-wired or is a cultural add-on is not always clear: there is so much pro-thin propaganda in our society that many men (and women) probably can't tell whether they are toeing the line in order to fit in, or really mean it. Nevertheless, for a variety of reasons a man may plunge into love with a woman who is curvier, more full-figured, or heavier than what he deems correct. Let's assume, for the sake of argument, that she is healthy, active, and fit, and her body type is simply natural to her.

What then happens is: whether the guy tries to be nice or not, the woman comes to realize that in his eyes she is not prized. This can happen because he doesn't compliment her, even when she is at her hottest; or because of the type of woman that he *does* stare at, on TV or on the street. Or he may tease her with her failure to measure down, thus betraying his careless belief that his own personal tastes are somehow universal.

It's hard enough for such a woman to like her own body *even if her partner adores it*, given the remorseless din of "information" on TV and in magazines with the sole (commercial) purpose of persuading every single woman on the planet, no matter how slim, that she needs to lose weight. But many women manage this anyway, celebrating their natural shapes and strutting their stuff, and even the culture seems to be starting to lighten up about it.

(Of course, the situation can be exactly reversed, as to body type or as to gender. A man who is addicted to curves may give his partner trouble because she doesn't have them. A woman who is slim may run her man down for being stocky.)

The best thing all of us can do, in addition to accepting ourselves the way our genes designed us, is to choose a partner who delights in that design. Unsolicited admiration is a very nice ally to self-esteem.

No matter what your healthy shape and size, there are going to be lots of folks out there who think you're just ducky. Men's tastes are just as varied as women's: it simply isn't true that everyone is looking for some one type. So next time around, find someone who is looking for you.

Body type was just one example. Natural appeal to one's partner is just as important in other areas:

- **Looks in general.** Whether we're talking face, fashion, or physique, it's easier to maintain a sense that one is attractive in the presence of a beholder who gets it.

- **Sexual performance.** A good recipe for keeping your sexual gusto is to be with someone who is highly susceptible to your moves, and who consciously craves what you are. It's no fun feeling like a bad lover, because you shared a bed with someone who needed someone else.

- **Humor.** Again, you can't condemn a person for not laughing at your best witticisms, but you don't need to be *with* that person. People can't help what strikes them funny; it is as essential a part of them as their bone marrow—maybe more essential, because it reflects not only the soul they were born with, but all the joys and sorrows of the road they've been on. If your last man made you feel less funny every year; if life itself lost the great resource of humor; then do a little forensic analysis and learn to detect the problem next time. Here are some questions to ask:

  · Was he able to make you laugh at yourself when that would have really helped? All of us have times when we take ourselves too seriously; to be deflated by a loving friend is the best medicine there is.

· Think of specific times when you said something that should have been hilarious, but it fell flat. Think about the content. Usually there is some crucial lesson lurking there.

· Think of instances when your partner laughed uproariously, and you saw nothing funny. Again, scrutinize the content. It may speak volumes about the distance between you as people.

False take-aways

The list goes on, of areas in which one partner can "disappoint" the other. The false take-aways abound: as well as unsexy and unfunny, you can end up feeling stupid, clumsy, or annoying, incompetent or slow, phony, or wishy-washy... and the cause of the problem is simply that you installed a critic in your life, whose notions of quality you were perfectly designed to flunk. What a good thing to avoid next time.

the professional abuser

Some people would try to sabotage *anyone* they were paired with. Whether they come from a long line of mistreatment, or just got it in the DNA lottery, doesn't matter—they need and want to hurt their mate. They need to undermine the other person's opinion of themselves, in order to maintain their own. It is how they get to feeling better.

Getting entangled with this kind of person endangers one's self-confidence and self-worth (as well as one's chances of happiness and, in extreme cases, one's life). Not that it's easy to leave. In more dire cases, to extricate oneself may require professional help, before, during and after.

On our grid of compatibility, such a person belongs on the margin. He is not compatible with anyone.

Even in its less overt forms, this sort of behavior should be a red flag. When you're getting to know a new person, it's good to take a zero-tolerance attitude towards it. Affectionate teasing can be delicious, but when you feel yourself being cut up, and there is coldness or meanness or malice behind it, walk on.

energy

It isn't good if there's a chronic situation where one spouse is rarin' to go and hungry for more, and the other is spent. Different people—even in good health—just naturally have different-sized batteries, and it's better to be with someone whose fuel supply is similar to your own. This may have shown up in the sexual arena, or it could have been a matter of whether you wanted to do anything active after getting through your work day.

> Different people—even in good health—just naturally have different-sized batteries

A false take-away

I'll never fit with anyone because my energy level is too low.

sex

It's very important to some people to reach the heights in bed; and that calls for a partner who has similar styles, tastes, and desire levels. The more unusual a person's tastes, the more critical this may be. There are deal-breakers lurking in this area, and if you found out what some of them were, you are armed with precious knowledge.

Conventional wisdom has it that sex declines drastically for most married couples, but there's a sort of counter movement arising these days, at least in the trendy magazines. If a couple once had good sex, it seems grudging to think there aren't ways they could revive it again. I'll talk about that more in Chapter 20.

A more relevant question for present purposes: was the sex *ever* what you wanted, and if not, why not and how important is that to you in the scheme of things?

A false take-away
This person didn't enjoy me in bed and wasn't satisfied, so that means I'm a failure sexually.

life goals and agenda

To some extent these things are negotiable, and they can even change when the right two people find each other—sometimes the whole plan gets scrapped and redone, because in the bracing presence of each other you can't accept half-measures anymore.

Was your last relationship inspiring in that way? Did you feel like a team; did you make each other's plans better? Was there mutual support?

Or did your agendas clash?

careers and jobs

Different couples have different ideas about job and career. All may work out if the two people are good with each other's visions. Looking back at your last relationship, ask yourself if the bar was set high enough by each person to fulfill themselves and satisfy the other person? Was it set *too* high, so that someone's standards weren't being met? Or was it perhaps too high in the opposite way: someone wanted a career so big it precluded a life together?

For some couples the right level means being able to get by financially, and still have enough juice left to enjoy life. For others it may mean a more demanding definition of "success" and material prosperity: the right house, the right neighborhood, the right schools, and so on. How did these variables shake out for you the last time around? Have your needs and wants emerged more clearly? Have they changed?

A false take-away

My partner was never satisfied with my career, so I'll have to fix it if I want to be happy with someone.

money and debt

Like other life challenges, financial issues can be dealt with if you face them together, get whatever expert advice you need, and make a plan. Were you able to talk about these things honestly with your partner, take care of them, allocate tasks and responsibilities? This is an area where a lack of unity can be a *serious* red flag. Did it show up?

A false take-away

I need to lighten up about credit cards.

children

The first question is, did you agree on whether you *wanted* them? And when?

Supposing you did, then we arrive at the biggest challenge two people can face—raising children. That activity can expose incompatibility like nothing else.

It may happen this way: One spouse instinctively takes on more authority with the children than the other, and no one seems to be able to do anything about it, but the less dominant one finds their new status demeaning, and that begins to sow resentment. Or the two have different assessments of what it is to be responsible parents, and thus a clash of values emerges. Worst of all is when one parent is more perceptive about the kids and their developing minds, and the other parent doesn't get this stuff and takes on an air of stupidity in the eyes of all concerned.

The presence of children can also offer up all sorts of adversity, from cognitive to financial to medical to sudden "Acts of God," and if the parents are able to meet these situations with force and cohesion, it will make their union stronger; but if they can't, if one lags behind or cops out, the prospects aren't good. The gap that was hinted at in the pre-children relationship may explode into a real breach. It's just another proof that one should catch the signs early on, because if there is a fault line, children will make it show up.

Children raise the stakes in every area they touch. If you and your ex had a lot of conflict in this area, take a close look at it, because it will reveal a lot about what you didn't have in common as people.

A false take-away
I'm better off leaving child-rearing to couples who are good at it.

values

It's a nebulous term. Depending on your stance, it might mean anything from your relationship with Jesus Christ to your relationship with the illegal alien who is nailing shingles to your roof. It might mean how you feel about the garbage truck driving away from your curb or the President receding into history. It has to do with what you want your children taught in school or at home, what you want them to watch on TV, and how much time you want them to spend outside the house and free of adult supervision.

> Values might mean anything from your relationship with Jesus Christ to your relationship with the illegal alien who is nailing shingles to your roof.

Values concern how you think a family should behave, and whether you want your new family to resemble the one you came from.

Values are about right and wrong. Truth versus lying. Compassion versus indifference. And how the world works. The degree to which you are engaged in public issues—and the way you choose to deal with them—is an important index of who you are as a person. And that affects who you can be comfortable with as a partner.

Ask yourself: Were you able to converse with your mate about personal/political/spiritual issues? Were you able to air them out and talk them through, even when you didn't agree? Did your mate allot them the same importance, or lack thereof, as you did? If not, that will help you know what to look for next time.

Ideally, you should be able to find a bedrock in your partner that you can lean on and count on, a sanctuary away from all the bull, a place where it is easier for you to find your way, with the firm grip of another's hand. Most of us can't be Gandhi: we need a moral ally.

A false take-away
I can't expect a partner to care about the same issues I do.

food, fun, and entertainment

food

Many people treat food as a form of entertainment. They choose what to eat based on pleasure, while the voices of nutritionists echo in the distance. Others insist on eating in a healthy way, and make the astounding claim that flavor is thereby maximized.

Food can be a very significant meeting place for two people, and can raise some real issues.

The first issue is whether meals even exist in a couple's life. A lot of people skip breakfast or eat it on the fly; lunch is part of the work day; that leaves dinner as the main couple opportunity, but it often gets sucked into the downdraft of TV, takeout, or random snacking.

If two people do make the effort to share a meal recognizable as "dinner," that raises more questions. Who prepares the food? Who cleans up? Who chooses the menu? On the first two, lots of different answers can be fair and balanced, but in many cases the chronic outcome is anything but.

How did it work out in your last relationship? Did you end up doing all the work? Did that rankle? Was your work at least *appreciated*? As far as menu goes, the more you care about nutrition and quality, the more likely you are to need a partner who cares too, and whose beliefs don't conflict with yours. Did you have that?

It takes dedication to buy healthy food and plan interesting meals, and it sometimes takes willpower to avoid the naughty temptations that could undermine the program. If one person isn't onboard, they can easily sabotage the other. Did that happen to you?

A good meal enjoyed with good conversation—whether it's in a restaurant or at home—is one of the prime attractions on the marquee of couplehood. It can be one of the reasons two people are glad to be a couple! It's also one of the best ways to avoid drifting apart. If you agree, then ask yourself how often this kind of occasion was achieved, last time around. If seldom, what stood in the way?

You have a right to look for a partner with whom food will be a positive, fun thing, a celebration, a collaboration and a meeting place—if that's what you want. Don't be afraid this area is somehow trivial; take stock of it when you're getting to know a man.

A false take-away

I've got to stop obsessing on nutrition!

fun and entertainment

Since work time is usually not spent together, play time had better offer some chances to bond. So it matters whether there are forms of recreation that you and your mate share.

Conversation is number one: if you don't have it you'll end up with nothing. Then there's a spate of others: games, physical and mental; socializing; outings of all kinds, from shopping to just going for a drive; art, music, films, TV; walking, running, working out; more active sports like hiking, fishing, boating, camping; summer retreats; travel; the list is endless. Did you and your partner find a decent number of these that you could enjoy together?

On the domestic front, the list narrows to the things you really do on most days.

Like television. One woman with no interest in sports told me that her memory of her first marriage was basically a bunch of men sitting in the living room watching "the game," whatever it happened to be, all weekend, and her job was to keep them fed. The roar of the crowd, the announcers yelling over that, and the guys yelling over *that*, were inescapable. They still echo in her brain as a nightmare that she will do anything to avoid in future, a way of living that she now clearly sees is incompatible with her own.

Television is in fact such a potent and perilous thing, that I will give it its own section, when we look at the ways that even well-matched couples go astray. I think unless wrestled into submission, it can do a lot of mischief.

A false take-away

I have this tendency to want to find leisure activities that my spouse and I both enjoy. But that's just being needy—most couples are more independent.

We've now picked our way through some juicy examples of incompatibility. There are others—the subject is rich—but I hope you've seen enough to realize that this process works. It's nothing less than an active reconstruction of the past. Cheerfully discarding the spurious messages that a mismatch tried to dictate, you take your own reading on what happened, and extract your own lessons about what you want in a future partner. The number one error laid to rest is that of thinking something was wrong with you, when you were really just with the wrong person.

To round out our survey of mismatch specifics, there are two *general* trends that need to be recognized as red flags—the chameleon response and the choice of bad boys.

the chameleon response

This arises when you make so many adjustments and changes in yourself, in order to fit with the man you've found, that you are in effect *forcing compatibility*. I talked earlier about loss of identity in a mismatched relationship, but I had in mind mostly the sacrifice of parts of yourself that the other person didn't like. The Chameleon Response is a more active thing. It means adopting a whole set of passions, interests, and allegiances just because the other person has them. It is changing your color to suit the situation.

Cindy learned to make Lance's BLT perfectly, and discovered a love inside herself for it!

Take the wedding. The bride is more spiritual than religious, but the groom's family is religious. So they want a big church wedding. So she caves, and allows the biggest day of her life to be mounted with words, songs, and rituals that she doesn't believe in. To complete the Chameleon Response, she actually makes herself, and him, and everybody else think that she now does believe in the Holy Trinity, the transmutation of the bread and the wine, and all the rest of it. Especially herself.

Not stopping at this, the chameleon may actually *change* religions in order to fit the bill. A Protestant may become Catholic; a Christian may become a Jew. It would seem an unlikely coincidence that a soul's take on ultimate reality could change just when it was romantically convenient, but life is full of surprises.

And this just scratches the surface. Or the depths.

When Cindy met Lance, she knew she wanted to be with him, and she quickly found out that he was a very outdoorsy guy. So just like that, she became a very outdoorsy girl. She espoused hiking and camping and climbing. She told him she loved these things. He wondered why she didn't have any of the equipment; she said she used to but was rusty, because her last boyfriend hadn't been interested. Cindy barely eluded serious injury on a number of occasions, before she learned enough to get by.

Lance liked to talk dirty during sex. Cindy allowed that she, too, found this stimulating.

Lance dressed preppie. Cindy, who had actually been a bit of a free spirit, went out and got a more constricted wardrobe.

Lance liked to eat the same sandwich for supper every day; a BLT on white toast made with a certain brand of bacon, a certain amount of iceberg lettuce, a certain thickness of tomato slice, unto death. Cindy learned to make this perfectly, and discovered a love inside herself for this same repast!

At some point, the backlash came, and blindsided the hapless Lance. Several years of dissimulation just detonated and Cindy became sarcastic, making sublime fun of every aspect of Lance's life. He was nonplussed. She broke free.

Whether in a mild or extreme form, this tendency to change or distort oneself in order to fit someone else's bill is a sure sign of a mismatch. Check it out in your past, and look at the specific ways in which you may have compromised yourself . . . they are inducements to resist next time.

bad boys

Do you have a habit of picking guys who aren't good for you? Many women have told me that they kick themselves for always choosing the "bad boy," the one who is naughty and sexy and a little danger-ous. One woman, Cassie, told me the following dramatic tale.

There was a reptilian coolness to his tongue.

In her late twenties, at the height of her dark, waifish beauty, she dated a guy named Bill for a year. Bill was a stable, hard-working, intelligent, warm, healthy, generous, burly, blue-eyed, honest fellow. He was a landscaper and Cassie was an in-terior decorator. Bill adored Cassie and maybe that was the problem. She liked him, but she had a rebel streak. She was restless—life seemed too smooth, the path to happiness too predictable. Sex with him was actually very good; there was no shortage of orgasms; but she could just see the three kids and the nice country house in their future.

Then one night when she went out with the girls, she met a guy at a dance club.

Matt was a tall, long-haired, dissolute-looking guy who wore a black duster. It emerged that he was a jazz piano player who also sold cars. He came on strong and his banter was edgy and quick. She let him kiss her and there was an unhurried, reptilian coolness to his tongue. He held her body not hungrily, but in a sort of appraising way, as if he was fingering fabric for a costume.

She sensed that he had illicit designs on her, that this wasn't going to be the road most traveled by. So she started an affair with Matt. He didn't disappoint her in the kink department. Their sex always seemed to be about power, and she liked the way they could trade roles and try to vanquish each other. It was a novelty; highly entertaining.

Cassie was still seeing Bill, but Bill was no fool. He sensed that something was wrong, that her attention was diluted. He called her on it. She told him she wasn't feeling it anymore and they broke it off. Bill cried at the end, but he accepted her verdict in a straight-forward Bill way.

Cassie committed to Matt, they moved in together, and things went well for a while. But one day when he didn't know she had come home, she overheard him making fun of her professional design work. He was on the phone, telling someone that Cassie's room colors reminded him of baby food. A small rift ensued, but it grew into a general feeling that they didn't see eye to eye. Matt thought she was too bourgeois. And she thought he was too flaky. It ended a few months later.

The coda: Years went by and Cassie found herself over forty and with a distinct children deficit. Then on a business trip she ran into Bill, who had moved to another city after they broke up. They had a drink in the hotel bar and Cassie got some very clear impressions. Bill was still a lovely man, still full of life and enthusiasm, and suddenly the things she had taken for granted were rare and precious in her eyes. She could tell he still found her attractive; but on her side it was worse—she was wildly, hopelessly smitten. She listened to his wry laughter about his three kids—he was divorced and had custody—and about his too-flourishing landscaping business, and she loved him.

She thought to herself, "This guy is so much smarter than Matt. I *had* this guy."

Bill called her room later that night. He wanted to know if she might want to meet for breakfast. Apparently there were no hard feelings about the past. But it emerged, the next morning, that there were lots of feelings about the future. Cassie didn't pass up her second chance.

Some of the things that Bad Boys offer aren't so bad. There's nothing wrong with a little danger, nothing wrong with chemistry. Bad Boys (and Girls) are a reminder that love should be a kick, it should sizzle. Especially when you're young, who wants to be respectable and complacent? At that age there's nothing worse than boredom. And fear is one of the great cures, with its mates, danger and risk.

But there are other cures that crop up later, like meeting an impossible deadline on a job you care about, or taking care of your loved ones. And there are other aphrodisiacs.

The thing is, badness can be overrated. Just how dangerous do you want your boy to be?

- Do you want him to leave the baby alone while he goes out to a strip joint?

- Do you want him to smoke in bed?

- Do you want him to lose the credit card invoices?

- Do you want him to chop salad veggies on the same board where he prep'd some raw chicken?

A lack of concern for consequences becomes much less charming when you have more to lose.

Maybe what we all want is the right combo of the scary and the safe, the naughty and the nice. But it's worth bearing in mind that within many a Bruce Wayne, there may lurk a Batman.

16

bewitched, bothered, and bewildered

love's crazed chemicals: are they irresistible?

$\mathcal{W}$e've explored the ins and outs of compatibility, and the value of it has shone brighter and brighter as we've surveyed its many varieties. But there's still a hitch. It won't do us any good to be clued in about compatibility, if we continue to choose our mates in a contrary way.

In our world, over forty percent of marriages end in divorce. A major reason for this, in my opinion, is that a lot of people are being drawn into Scenario A: choosing partners with whom they aren't well matched.

How does this happen? Let's take a typical couple and ask them. "Looking back, now that it's over, how did you get with someone who wasn't right for you? You obviously believed at the start that they were the one; but given the way things turned out, there must have been clues that you didn't really have enough in common. Or at the very least, there can't have been much evidence that you did.

"So how did the whole thing get launched? What possessed you to choose that person?"

The answer they're likely to give is, "We fell in love."

And that's all they need to say. Because we understand that feeling. Everyone knows that falling in love is a captivating impulse, hard to question and hard to resist. Yet if we look around, the evidence is everywhere that this aura, this feeling, cannot be trusted to lead to happiness. People rely on the magic of being in love and they get burned. Real compatibility plays second fiddle and a more serious, lasting kind of love doesn't have a chance. It's as if the in-love sensation is a runaway team of horses; the stagecoach driver has lost control of them and they are pulling the relationship to disaster.

In this and the next chapter I want to break the hold of this belief system, and show how we can regain the reins of romance, and use compatibility to steer the coach. The only way to do that is to take a new look at this peculiar experience that is called *falling in love*. We are so familiar with it that we can't see it. So I'm going to ask:

- What is falling in love? How does it feel?

- Is it irresistible?

- Why does it exist? What is its purpose on this planet? Is it hardwired into us?

- Do we sometimes abuse it?

- How can we best use it?

I believe that by answering these questions, we can figure out how to harness this powerful force, and bring it under the influence of the valuable lessons we've learned along the way—about things like overcoming the wounded ego, avoiding rebound logic, upholding the self, and honoring compatibility.

To get started, let's get a fresh reading on the raw experience.

this is your brain on love

Greg got a new job in mid-life. He was downsized from management in a once-healthy corporation and had to move into work he didn't really like that much, in marketing for a major hotel chain. He turned fifty in his new cubicle, in a row that was untouched by sunlight. The people who worked in his area brought a cake. Motley but nice, they helped him adjust and learn the ropes.

And they warned him about Shannon, the supervisor. They said, don't trust her and don't be too open with her. She is disorganized and she is a backstabber. She always butters up new people, because she craves attention and the veterans are onto her. But don't tell her any problems you are having, because after the honeymoon period, she will use them against you. (They didn't think of her as having any allure, so they didn't warn against that.)

He felt like a young pony in a garden of peyote.

Greg had been alone for nearly a decade. After a bad breakup he had sworn off love for years; later, loneliness made him try dating a couple of women, but nothing had developed yet.

Then he set eyes on Shannon and his world was rocked. He couldn't exactly say why. She was certainly not put together. She was oblivious to moments when her top didn't close the gap to the back of her skirt; her hair was a nest of snakes; her complexion was by turns pale and torrid. She shouldn't have been appealing, but somehow her style violations cracked open his own protective layer. And that light in her eyes, like the glint of steel, unseated him.

He had to work with her on several difficult cases that he couldn't solve himself. He found himself sitting right next to her, in his cubicle or hers. And her physical proximity did something unholy to him. It wasn't exactly lust he felt. It was more like madness. He felt as if he was on laughing gas when she was close to him. He could

hardly attend to her instructions, which were rapid-fire and complicated and on which his future hung. Even if they were discussing the
twenty-seventh workaround in the company software, he heard the
chirping of birds in the springtime.

He was losing it. He started looking forward to every time Shannon
(who resided on a different floor) would come into the room. When
he heard her voice talking to someone else, he listened like a teenager
to detect whether she liked that person better than him. When she
entered his cubicle he was in a lather. When she flirted with him, as
she did very openly with his co-workers listening, he was reckless and
rakish in his responses. She knew he had been an executive in his previous job, and she acted awed by his presence. Maybe she really felt
that, at the beginning: maybe she had a crush on him too.

No wonder lovers have one-track minds.

But she was volatile and task-
oriented and, in her scattered way,
ferociously loyal to the company—
and ferociously ambitious. And she
was tough. So Greg's abject focus on her was only sporadically returned. And that just drove him crazier.

One day she was cross with him, for not paying attention during
one of her explanations. He was mortified and went to the bathroom,
his heart pounding. When he came back she was being very cozy
with another recent hire and he was so jealous he couldn't think.
Then in the late afternoon she was nice to him again and he nearly
danced across the parking lot after work.

While driving home he would argue with himself. Do I tell
Shannon how I am feeling? Will it blow my job? What if she isn't
feeling the same way? Then he would tell himself he was nuts. It
could never work out; he could never deal with a person so high
maintenance. And Shannon was attached (she constantly made fun
of her husband to anyone who would listen). Yet something in him

wanted to declare himself to her. The compulsion was extreme. It was as if he wanted to throw everything he had at her feet, as an offering, a tribute to show what she did to him.

The worst thing was wanting to kiss her. She did have a beautiful face and sometimes when she was inches from him, he nearly couldn't restrain himself.

He had not felt this way for years. He had not thought that he *could* still feel this way. He was fifty. He was staid. He was stable. Now he felt like a young pony in a garden of peyote.

Three times he almost went over the edge. But he somehow held back.

Then on a hectic Wednesday, at an all-hands meeting, Shannon tore into him, savaged his metrics in front of the team, accused him of disregard for the protocols and the schedule, and said he was not mastering the software. He blurted out a lame answer to the first charge, then lost his bearings and couldn't separate what was true in her words from what was false. His comrades stared at him, not happy to see their predictions borne out.

From that day she was the enemy and he had to use all his brain power to recover the ground he had lost and defend himself against her. All his feelings for her disappeared overnight and his concentration, now restored, served him well in battle. He hung on to his job.

But he had come close, so close, to disaster.

Greg asked himself, *What happened to me? What was I in the grip of?* When he saw Shannon now, he felt no attraction, no excitement, no impulse to kiss her. None of those things. It wasn't just that he was mad at her now and disliked her. He was also indifferent to her as a woman. He saw nothing in her that would make him want to trade his life away. Had the whole thing been a hallucination or what?

At best we would have to say Greg was in a drug-addled state. Scientists report that they are beginning to identify real changes in the brain that accompany new love. Significant neural regions light up like city blocks; exotic chemicals like dopamine and norepinephrine course around and trip emotional switches, subjecting us to a bewildering mixture of feelings. Even unto madness: one of the chemical signatures of *amour* may be also associated with obsessive-compulsive disorder. No wonder lovers have one-track minds. Some scientists also believe that people emit pheromones which can drive the right recipient wild; maybe that that was part of how Shannon got to Greg.

So what have we learned from Greg's story? It illustrates three important points:

1. **The state of being in love is baffling and powerful.** Baffling because it conjures up a bizarre combination of emotions, including euphoria, desire, excitement, adoration, dreaminess, jealousy, hilarity, reckless audacity, worship, and loss of one's rational faculties, well described in a song called "Bewitched, Bothered and Bewildered", a mixture that comes together under no other human circumstance. Powerful because it trains this arsenal on a single person of our acquaintance and impels us to grant this person a special status in our lives. It's a potent witches' brew, a chemical recipe that plunges us into a unique strain of madness.

2. **It's dangerous, the In-love Reaction.** What makes it dangerous is that it can so easily be aroused by an inappropriate person and then can wreak havoc in a person's life. If Greg had succumbed to what he was feeling, there is little doubt that he would have ended up with a broken heart and a lost job. Shannon's true colors would have emerged sooner or later.

And this result is in no way atypical, given how many relationships go awry.

Think how odd this really is. Most of the intense reactions that nature has built into us have an obvious and immediate utility. When you eat tainted meat, your body rises up in revolt, wracking you to get rid of the contaminated agent. When a pebble heads for your eye, the lid closes faster than thought. When a doctor taps on your knee with her little rubber mallet, your leg obligingly kicks up, thus preventing you from failing the physical.

"I'm supposed to believe that's when humans first began to fall in love? Only nine hundred years ago?"

So why this life-disrupting impulse to join your fortunes to another's, so often provoked by the wrong object? As we saw in the last chapter, a successful romantic relationship requires that two people get it on in a whole bunch of areas, including sex, personality, emotional makeup, life goals and agenda, culture, and values.

So it would have behooved the Darwinian forces that shaped our genes to delay the In-love Reaction until these matters could be investigated. Romance would run a lot more smoothly if it went like this: you find someone attractive, then you get to know them in all their aspects, test how they fit with you, and only at the moment when the brain comes up with a finding of "compatible" does the In-love Reaction kick in.

We aren't designed that way; but fortunately there is a saving grace . . .

3.   **The In-love Reaction can be resisted.** You don't have to give into it. Greg didn't, and that is a major moral of his story. True,

he was rescued from his thralldom before his rational mind completely crumbled, saved by his beloved's timely abuse of him. Would that we were all that lucky when cupid lashes us to a disastrous partner.

But my point is that when some of the real estate in our brains is captured by the love god, that doesn't mean the whole organ is captured. We have enough brain terrain still in our control that one portion can resist the other. Even before Shannon turned into a viper, Greg could clearly see that what he was feeling was ridiculous. He couldn't stop feeling it, but he could enclose it in a sort of rational quarantine.

It's kind of like being stoned on a hallucinogen (so I hear). The cops riding by on their motorcycles may look to you like flesh-eating zombies from a horror movie, but that doesn't mean you can't stop yourself from pulling out your gun and shooting them.

A person in the grip of infatuation can decide that isn't who they want to be with.

The failure to resist the In-love Reaction is part of the story of how a lot of bad relationships got started. The rest of its mischief we'll see in the very next chapter.

But first, in order to get a further handle on the power of romantic love, we need to ask: is it something we learn from our culture, or has it always been part of the human animal? Just how deeply entrenched is this menace? Put another way . . .

how old is love?

As I type these words I feel two hands on my shoulders, and there's a female voice close to my ear. I have been concentrating so hard I didn't notice that someone was eavesdropping on my work.

Yes, I've wandered into that bar again. I feel I should explain myself. I do most of my writing in a solitary room with one window, but on some days when the paragraphs are flowing, it feels good to take them for an outing. This restaurant bar is nice in the afternoon, quiet and cool, with a view of the bustling street. It's near the university; you can see people with books. A clean, well-lighted place. A good place to drink espresso until your writing is done.

My female companion says, "Love is not built into human beings. It was invented in the late eleventh century."

That century thing always throws me. "You mean the late 1000s?" I say, beginning to guess who I'm talking to. She steps up beside me and I see that indeed, it's Ms. Professor.

Only she looks different. Her eyes are bright. Her dark hair is down from its bun, swept to one side like an actress from the forties. She is wearing a purple dress that accentuates her slender waist—a feature which escaped my notice that first time we met. I'm getting a Bette Davis vibe.

"I do," she says.

It takes me a moment to remember what she's replying to. Oh yes.

I say, "So I'm supposed to believe that's when humans first began to fall in love? Only nine hundred years ago?"

"No, that's when they first began to tell *stories* about falling in love. That was the preliminary step. Intricate poems, sung by wandering troubadours in the south of France."

"I've heard of the Courtly Love tradition," I say a little crossly. "But I find it hard to believe that it all started so late in human history—in medieval times. What did people do before that?"

"Well, they did have sex."

"I wondered."

"And they felt love, but that was for friends and family, and God. But then the troubadours' stories caught on, and real people began to imitate them . . . until it became part of our culture. Which it still is. I saw a flavor of it in your Greg story."

"You did?"

"I've been here awhile. Yes, when you talked about how he wanted to lay everything at Shannon's feet. That is very 'Courtly Love'. You said he was in awe of her, worshiped her, became rakish and reckless. The courtiers felt that way about the grand ladies they admired. And they went through sweet anguish when their love was not returned."

At this point I see Bar Guy come in. I wave to him, but instead of approaching us, he goes around to the far side of the horseshoe-shaped bar and sits by himself, gazing off in another direction.

"What's with him?" I say, remembering that they seemed to hit it off last time.

"Oh, he's afraid of me," she says, and her eyes flash merrily.

"So—the unrequited thing," I say. "That was a big part of Courtly Love, I'm thinkin'."

"Yes, some scholars think that was the real core of what they invented. The poetry of non-consummation."

"All these knights never got to sleep with these princesses?"

"That isn't perfectly clear," she says. "In some poems it goes only as far as hugging and kissing; in some it gets very hot and heavy. And in a lot of them, it remains chaste. One brave knight never meets his love object at all!"

"That's a true long-distance relationship."

Ms. Professor has been studying Bar Guy. "Jerome looks flummoxed," she says. "I'm going to have to go talk to him." Her tongue visits her upper lip.

"Wait!" I say. "I want to bounce something off you."

"Bounce away." But she gets off her stool.

"Well, I think if you look at classical literature, the Bible and so on, or if you just think about human nature, this in-love thing is just too basic to have been invented in the Middle Ages. Are we supposed to think every great coupling before that was purely sexual?"

"You may have a point," she says. "I was being devil's advocate. I have to go."

"There is new evidence in the brain books," I say. "Aren't you aware of it? They say romantic love is hard-wired into us."

"I've heard about this," she says. "I haven't had time to look into it, but off the top of my head, I think they're speculating."

She glances restlessly over at Bar Guy.

"I really have to go talk to Jerome," she says. "By the way, I don't think we ever . . . I'm Abigail."

She shakes my hand, and I tell her my name.

She nods to me and heads around the bar.

Alone again, I think about the brain. Helen Fisher says in her book, *Why We Love*, that science has now amassed enough evidence to say that romantic love is a basic drive, built into our genes. It isn't avoidable, or cultural; it's instinctive. That would certainly help explain why the In-love Reaction is so strong. And how it can shape a person's whole life, impose an agenda.[1]

It still doesn't explain why it chooses its objects so carelessly.

I look across the bar and I see that there are developments between Bar Guy and Ms. Professor. Abigail is *necking* with Jerome. I wonder how long this has been going on.

Keeping my writerly concentration, I think about other "involuntary" reactions. Everyday ones.

Laughter. A rippling orgasm of insight that shakes the belly and causes us to widen our mouths, exhale violently, and bray like

---

1. Fisher's book *Why We Love* (2004) is a fascinating treatment of the evolutionary functions and brain bases of romantic love, which summarizes a lot of material and boldly proposes new theory.

donkeys. I think about anger. What it does to the body and the mind, all tied together and obviously deeply imbedded in our DNA. I think about tears.

And then it occurs to me, you can work yourself up into these states, when you really want to. You can *induce* them.

Could that be true of falling in love?

17

did you fall or
did you jump?

love as a plunge into the irrational

$\mathcal{L}$ove is dangerous enough when it blindsides us, and unexpectedly we find ourselves in its clutches, spellbound by a certain someone and eating our hearts out. Its force isn't easy to resist, and that's why many of us have succumbed and ended up in relationships with the wrong people.

It's more fun to put all your bucks on an unknown horse than to follow the Racing Form.

But what is harder to condone is a more perverse phenomenon—*plunging into love as a deliberate way to slip the leash of common sense.* We humans are capable of a lot of mischief, and maybe one of our best tricks is to purposely wrap ourselves in the fog of romance, in order to do something foolish.

Now what circumstance would provoke such behavior? Maybe this.

The Life Alarm rings and it's time for a relationship. The moment is ripe, but there's a glitch: the only candidate we've found isn't really right for us. We need a way to

paper over that fact so we can move forward. We need
a form of delusion. So we induce the state of being in
love; we use it as a gambit to allow us to move our agenda forward.

And fortunately, we have several things on our side.

One, recklessness carries its own unique rush. Facing a major decision, people sometimes take the attitude of "the less I know, the
better!" It's more fun to put all your bucks on an unknown horse than
to follow the Racing Form. Even cold-blooded corporate types can
be caught doing this: you'll see them overlook a long-time employ-
ee who has earned the corner office, in order to bring in somebody
they know squat about, based on a slick resume and a steamed-
up interview.

Two, there's a very popular theory that love *should* be mad and
impetuous. That's the genius of it, that's the height of the romantic.
In *A Midsummer Night's Dream* Shakespeare groups together "the lu-
natic, the lover and the poet," saying that "lovers and madmen have
such seething brains" that they overshoot "cool reason". Many people take this as a *recommendation*.

But is it?

taylor's deadline

Taylor was an aspiring actress of thirty-three, a blonde southern belle
who found herself at a less-than-stellar point in her still-young life.
She had a rich dad, a self-made industrial magnate who had financed
her thespian efforts, and she had gotten on a commercial for the
pharmaceutical industry's latest discovery, Bad Dream Syndrome. She
played the sympathetic wife whose husband was having nightmares.
She suggested he try this new drug called Oblivan. The voice-over
said its side effects included nausea, double vision, itchy feet, and

insomnia, but he was seen sleeping blissfully as she watched over him in the middle of the night.

However, no bigger offers seemed to be forthcoming. A couple years ago Dad had even funded an independent movie, which against Taylor's better lights he also ended up directing, but it got rejected by Sundance. So what was Taylor to do?

She had had one serious relationship with a man but it hadn't worked out. Rick was a struggling screenwriter, a talented one—it was his script that her dad had produced—but her father had convinced her that he wasn't a team player.

The last thing she needed was to learn some nuisance detail that might threaten the whole deal.

Taylor badly needed a distraction. And the one that came to mind was to be able to flash a ring and talk about her good fortune. So she went on eHarmony, did the one-hour quiz and asked them to locate her soulmate.

Soon they did. Brandon was a man of twenty-seven who lived two thousand miles away and shared her fundamentalist Christian faith (or was it her dad's?). He was good-looking, judging by his photos, and he had money. He worked for his father, a real estate tycoon who owned part of a major league team.

Brandon's emails were very upbeat, and she sensed that she could escape the angst that her career and her ex had thrust upon her, and propel herself into a world where things were cheerful.

They met in Brandon's city, where there were palm trees and an ocean, and she fell for him at first sight. He was smooth-skinned, impish, unruffled by life, ready to wear the right clothes to the right parties forever. He took her for a dreamy sailboat ride on the Pacific. They played tennis and swam in his dad's pool and they made love in the lavish guest house where he lived, on his dad's estate. The sex was as perfect as the manicured lawn.

They got engaged the second time they met. Taylor entered a state of constant euphoria. Her life back home improved immensely. Her posse was enchanted by Brandon, her status was through the roof and her life had a winning storyline. It was that storyline that she clung to; she didn't want to hear anything that could possibly disturb it. She really believed that Brandon was her prince and that was good enough for her. Her explanation of her good luck was simple—she had needed this to happen and therefore it had! (It didn't occur to her that was the *only* reason it had happened . . .)

The fact that he lived so far away only added to Brandon's charm, because there was not the danger of finding out too much about him. Facts she saw as a hazard. They couldn't make things any better—because things were perfect—but they could possibly cause trouble. The last thing she needed was to learn some nuisance detail that might threaten the whole deal. She was like a home buyer who is smitten with a certain property, and doesn't want it to be inspected by a professional.

On the wedding day it was hot and humid in the antebellum mansion. She and her lover had a faint patina of sweat on their smiling faces as the minister led them through the vows. She had taken a tranquilizer because she was a little overwrought.

The honeymoon in the Caymans was curiously blank; Taylor felt that they needed more people around them. Not a lot of sex took place. Not a lot of conversation. She tried to engage him but he seemed less verbal than she had thought.

She had agreed to live at his place for the time being, and her stuff had been moved there. When they walked into the bedroom, all her accessories were beautifully arrayed. She opened a walk-in closet and her clothes and shoes were on display. The surprise was what he said next: "Now do you want to see *my* bedroom?"

Brandon's lifestyle was the next surprise. It turned out he didn't really work for his dad. He didn't really have a job. It was more that he had an allowance, and he occasionally did errands. What he *mostly* did was to hang out at the marina with a bunch of perky guys who did a little sailing and a lot of drinking. Then this same crew would repair to his dad's basement where there was a video emporium, and they would spend hours competing with each other.

Taylor missed her friends back home. She especially found herself thinking about her ex, Rick, and about all the deep conversations they used to have, concerning acting and screenwriting and life. They hadn't always agreed, but they had certainly engaged with each other.

Taylor tried to organize some auditions in nearby L.A., but it was an uphill battle. She spoke to Brandon about her challenges and he seemed uninterested. When she pressed him for feedback, he said, "Don't you think you're a little old to try to break in as an actress?"

That led to a serious rift, and when the time was right, Brandon brought her flowers and then brought up the idea of them having children. That had been her total dream, but now she asked herself, "Do I *want* to have children with this guy?" And the answer was all too clear.

Taylor hit bottom. She had thrown herself into the shiny waters of love, and under the surface had hit cold, sharp rocks. It was time to call this one off.

When she got back home, she caught a faint look of relief on her father's face. It was clear, he was glad to have his little girl back in the castle.

A few days later she called Rick. "We need to talk," she said.

So there you have it—love as a plunge into the irrational.

Clearly it's not the best place to take this emotion. To treat falling in love as a delightful dip into delusion may be fine for a while, but under the pressure of a day-to-day life together (let alone children) it is bound to be tested and it will break down, if it only has that component.

Love should be the marriage of the rational (friendship) and the non-rational (sex); but it shouldn't be *irrational*.

An interesting gloss on this was given to me by a woman who helps run a world-class wedding venue. She sees hundreds of different bridal couples pass through the halls and the fascinating thing is that she has developed the ability to tell which duos are going to succeed. One of the marks of the ones who won't survive is that they are way too caught up in the symbolism and artifice (and material status trappings) of the whole thing, and way too stressed by the logistics. Will the flower displays be exactly right? Will it rain?

They're stressed out by whether the symbolism is going to hold together, because they have no substance to cling to. That's because the other person is a cipher to them: they have made a plunge into the unknown and are trying desperately to hide from that fact. The couples who really know and like each other—who are true friends—are different. They sail through any hitches, laughing them off; they aren't worried about symbolism because their hopes are based on actual evidence.

the solution to the romantic love conundrum

So what are we to do with this thing I've called the In-Love Reaction, this altered state (as lofty as poetry and as deep as mating) that makes us exalt its object above all others, regardless of how inappropriate that object is?

Do we have to think of it as a threat to happiness—an enemy of compatibility?

Surprisingly, I think the answer is no. The key to this answer lies in the message carried by the experience of being in love. If we only think of its dangerous power to impel us, we neglect its avowed agenda, the thing it is reaching for. And paradoxical as it may sound, I think that thing is *union with a soulmate.*

That's what nature gets us all stirred up about; that's what makes us bewitched and bothered—the sense that this person we've met is the one who can be our lover *and* our best friend. That's why falling in love feels more monumental than simple sexual attraction. The whole emotional extravaganza is nature's way of telling us that life's biggest brass ring is at hand (the best chance for successful mating). When the chemicals kick in, that's exactly what they are saying.

What misfires is not the goal, which is noble and right. What goes wrong is that the In-love Reaction tends to make its move before it has collected enough information. It picks up a few facts about the new person, a few promising facts, then makes its leap, which is nevertheless an attempt to reach for something wholly worthwhile. The leap is in good faith, but it too often misses its own target. And if things then go awry, that isn't what the In-love Reaction had in mind.

For that reason I think it can be reasoned with. If we take the time to gather facts that affect the outcome it desires, it just might be willing to listen. I mean, compatibility (which equals soulmate-ness) is exactly what it is looking for—that is its specialty. So even though it is a magic spell, it may be amenable to data on *that* subject.

It's up to us. If we don't abuse the In-love Reaction by summoning it for specious reasons, and if when it arises naturally we take a little care to supply it with good information about whether we really have anything in common with the person under consideration, things just might work out okay. If confronted with clear evidence that its mission is going to fail, the In-love Reaction will spontaneously retreat (as in the case of Greg).

I'll admit it, there is a thrill to "loving across a gap." It's exciting to fall for someone you know very little about; it's especially kicky on a sexual level.

But you know what? It's exciting to fall in love with someone you love.

grounded love

I was a guest on a radio show in Calgary, Alberta, one snowy Tuesday during Valentine's week, when this point was made crystal clear. Listeners were supposed to call in and give their thoughts on Valentine themes, and the hostess and I were expecting a lot of calls from women, and a lot from young people. Instead what we got was over half the calls from men, middle-aged and older.

> But you know what? It's exciting to fall in love with someone you love.

These men wanted to tell us how blessed they felt, because decades earlier, they had found a wonderful woman. They wanted to talk about how they had met, and they kept using the phrase "my best friend." Many of these calls were very touching. But the ones that took the cake—and there were several of them—involved a special plot line.

> She and I were good friends for years. We each went through other relationships and it never dawned on us that we could be anything more than friends. Then we found ourselves both unattached at the same time, and we were spending a lot of time together, and really we'd become each other's best pals. And one day, one of us—I can't remember which—said, "You know, I've always found you attractive. I mean, do you think there's any way that . . . " And we looked at each other, and we

smiled, and a change took place, surprisingly fast; we
went to a whole other level. It was very romantic—very
sexy too. And by the time we realized what we had, we
realized that we had never had it with anyone else.

This story shows that there is a beautiful, positive way in which
the In-Love Reaction can be induced, encouraged, deliberately culti-
vated. And in a good way, it provides further proof that we have more
control over it than many claim. The terrifying forces that come into
play when you fall in love can actually be summoned in the service
of real compatibility.

And that is exactly what I recommend. When you meet an interesting person, enjoy the sensations that run through you, enjoy
the thrills on the midway ride. If it feels romantic and sexy, savor
that. But don't forget to try out the friendship side, the conversations
about every conceivable thing, the shared experiences as you try exploring the world together. And gently, firmly, hold a little piece of
your soul back. Fight the compulsion to throw all your chips on that
number, until you've had a chance to evaluate. Don't commit yet,
keep your eyes open and learn learn learn; find out if there is a real
foundation to build on.

And don't think that when you swear off the unsuited kind of
partner that you chose last time, that means you have to give up the
magic and romance too. In fact it is *more* romantic to fall in love with
someone you really like as a person, than with someone you have to
deceive yourself to fall for. **Grounded love is more romantic than
wishful love; clear-sighted love beats deluded love every time.**
And grounded love proves itself in another important way—it lasts.

There's one more thing we can do to give romantic love the best possible chance of being evoked by someone who is really worth it. That

is to give ourselves more choice of partners. Go out and make a real effort to meet the right person, instead of taking the passive approach and choosing only from those who happen to wash up on our shore. I wrote a whole book on this topic, *Why Mr. Right Can't Find You*, about the many opportunities that are available in today's world for those who are willing to be intrepid.

But there is one avenue I want to emphasize here, because history has turned a corner that makes grounded love much more possible than ever before. So when you are ready to look for a new relationship, consider this.

online dating as a plunge into the rational

In the good old days (less than two decades ago) most folks didn't have a very big selection of partners, and so they could be forgiven if they fell in love foolishly. Especially once they were out in the working world, it wasn't that easy to meet people, and who wanted to be lonely?

That's how it was, but it isn't that way anymore, because the Internet came along and changed the landscape of romance forever. The big frustration used to be knowing your dream mate was out there somewhere, but not being able to find them. Now all it takes is for both of you to be seriously looking online.

It should be obvious that if you have more candidates to choose from, you will make a better choice. But let me offer a simple proof. Suppose there are three men out there, A, B, and C, all of whom would find you attractive and interesting and would want to be with you, if they had the chance. Now suppose that if you met them, you would find A and B attractive physically, and you'd find B and C to be simpatico and friend material. If you only meet A and C, you'll have a tough choice, and you'll either end up alone or with a man who is only a partial match for you. But if you meet all three, you'll easily choose B. He wins over either of the others, *if you get a chance to meet him.*

This illustrates the power of choosing from more people. There are many good ways to achieve that. But it is the special genius of online mating.

Not only does the Internet give you much more choice, but the online interface encourages you, and in some ways forces you, to approach that choice in a more rational manner. And therefore it is more likely to lead to what I called *grounded love.* Let us count the ways.

1. If you go to a store and they only sell one kind of fridge, there's a tendency to just take it and get on with your day. Why learn a whole lot about it if you know you're going to buy it anyway? But if they sell five different kinds of fridge, you're going to ask the salesperson to point out the different features, explain the advantages and disadvantages—because how else can you choose? Greater selection demands greater knowledge; it forces you to do some research. It's exactly the same with online dating. If you are confronted with five worthy prospects, you're going to delve into their details, so you can decide which guy is right for you. You're going to do your homework before deciding which of them to meet in person. And what will you be looking for? Compatibility. What a good thing to do upfront.

2. When you're checking out people online, you have a few photos to look at and the rest is words.[1] You see their responses to multiple choice questions, and you read their own words in

---

1. On some sites you can also see a video introduction.

their profile, and then if there is mutual interest you probably end up emailing quite a bit and talking on the phone, before you meet in person. This has been well described as "getting to know people from the inside out." Under more traditional circumstances, when the first encounter is in person, it is much easier for people to get distracted by chemistry and sometimes short-circuit the process of getting to know someone's character and interests.

3. Choosing candidates to consider is very efficient online. Before you even look at individual ads you can use search parameters to find those who meet your criteria in areas like age range, body type (meaning you each like the other's), location, income, drinking and smoking preferences, politics, religion, desire for children, and many others. So you get the benefit of a large pool of people, while being able to narrow it down easily to the ones you will look at more closely.

4. When you go the online route, you are in control of your own presentation, in every detail. You can choose photos that represent you fairly and positively. You can decide exactly what to say about yourself. You can present your mind, your wit, your soul by creating a profile that expresses these things. And the more specific and original you are in your profile, the easier it is for your true mate to recognize you. When the first encounter was in person, it was often hard to get to the things that you wished the other person to know, and to find out the things about them that mattered to you. You didn't get to focus their attention on the facets of you that you wanted them to react to. Now you do.

Once you do meet in person with someone you discovered online, you may take to each other or you may not. You may have to check out quite a few people before you find a comfort level in being together, an ease of communication, passions in common, and passion in common too. When you find those things, magic may well happen. And if you conduct an online quest with skill and persistence, you've got a good chance that it will be *grounded* love.

18
abigail and jerome

I hadn't been to the bar for a couple of weeks. But one day after finishing my writing I went for a walk, and ended up there.

It was five in the afternoon, a bright, windy day in June. I ordered a Blue Moon and looked around. There wasn't anybody I knew except the bartender Grace, so I sat at a table by the window, opened a paper and read a movie review, with one eye on the street life.

I was interrupted by a face outside the window. It was Bar Guy, staring at me and looking urgent. I waved to him and he came in and stood near me.

"Hi, Jerome," I said.

"Hey, do you mind if I sit down with you?"

"Sure, come on. I wasn't doing anything."

He got a drink and brought it over. He asked me how my writing was going, and I said pretty well. What was I writing about? I said the merits of online dating.

"Really," he said, and he looked panicky. "I've been wanting to talk to you, you haven't been here."

"No, not since I saw you and Ms. Professor . . . "

"Kissing. I know." He looked chagrined. "That's what I wanted to talk to you about."

Sweat broke out on his forehead and he looked really distressed. I realized that I had never taken a good look at his face. I had typed him as sort of blond beachcomber type, but he wasn't, really. He had more of a workingman's angle to his shoulders, and something discerning in his blue eyes. He was wearing a white T-shirt, jeans, and boat shoes. And an analogue watch that looked old. Really old.

"So, what is going on?" I said.

"I think I'm in love with her," he said, and sat back, wiping his brow.

"Sounds okay," I said.

"It isn't! I'm really gone over her. I can't do this."

He looked like he was going to start crying. I sat forward and gave him big attention.

"She doesn't return the feeling?" I said.

"No, she does." He crumpled into silence again.

"Jerome, I don't know you very well, but you're gonna have to tell me what the problem is."

He made a gesture with his left hand, as if he was drawing a diagram on the table. "I'm not right for her," he said. "I'm not the right type. She's in a different league. I'm just a regular guy. I've tried this before and it was a disaster."

"Okay," I said. I had to applaud his caution. He was trying to control the In-Love Reaction long enough to take a look at things.

"I am getting what you're laying down," I said. "Relax, it isn't too late to do the right thing."

"I know. I can stop myself. It'll mean not seeing her anymore, not ever." He looked really upset at this thought.

"How much *have* you been seeing her?"

"A lot. A lot." He rubbed his hands together, as if to illustrate the contact. Then he leaned over to me and whispered, "I've never had sex like this in my life. I didn't know I could. With her it's like . . . cosmic." He laughed sheepishly, and I did too.

"But she's a professor," he went on, "and I didn't finish high school. I work with my hands. I might as well be somebody she would hire to do her yard work. That was the problem with my wife. She was rich and I just couldn't fit in."

As he sat there looking disconcerted, again I saw something in his eyes that seemed like really high intelligence. My heart went out to him and I thought, what if he's just scared? I decided to be the attorney for the defence.

> "So maybe that *wasn't* the problem between you and your wife."

"Is Abigail rich?" I said.

"Well, no."

"Are you?"

He looked startled. "Uh . . . maybe. I might be." He laughed.

I said, "So maybe that *wasn't* the problem between you and your wife."

"Okay, point taken. But she was classy. She had a *lot* of class. I'm not in that league."

"So now you have to avoid classy women? Like Abigail?"

"Right."

"Jerome, you don't seem to me like an unclassy guy. I see class in you." I laughed.

He looked embarrassed. "Okay, okay, I don't know what it is. Yeah, I do. Abigail is a frickin' intellectual. I mean, she is *smart*. Brilliant really. She's . . . out of sight."

"Okay, that's good, that's fresh ground. Let's look at that. I'm a little short on facts here. Let's start with, what do you do, exactly?"

"It's kind of complicated. My father and I have a business. We supply things for people who renovate old boats. Or recreate them."

"Old boats? I knew there was something nautical about you!"

He smiled. "I live on a houseboat. And we have a big workshop on the shore, used to be a warehouse. Part of it is for documents, part for tools, part for parts and materials. The foundry's in a separate building."

"You have a *foundry*?"

"We do. We have to create some of the fittings ourselves."

He explained to me what he and his dad were doing. People all over the country, and in other countries, were restoring antique boats: cigar-shaped launches, gorgeous yachts, even old-time steamboats. They needed replacement parts: engine parts, deck fittings, lights, wheels, the whole thing. They often had a portion of the original, but the rest was gone. Somebody had to create new molds and castings and pour metal and machine the result and in sum, come up with the missing pieces.

"So you manufacture history," I said.

"That's a good way of putting it. The original companies aren't there anymore, so we stand in for them."

"How can you do that?" I said. "How do you know the exact specifications?"

"Sometimes we have a model to duplicate. Sometimes we have to work from old photos or old diagrams. Or old descriptions. That's why we have the document collection. It's two thousand square feet of shelves. My grandfather started it; it won't stop growing."

I smiled. "So this is interesting," I said. "You basically have a library of boatbuilding history."

"Yeah, you could say that," he said. "But I carry a lot of it in my brain."

"I'll bet you do. I'll bet you do." I was lost in thought. This guy was like combination of an archeologist and an artisan.

"Do you work a lot with copper?" I asked.

"Sure. Brass too. Why?"

"I don't know. I just love copper." I looked at him quizzically. "Have you shown your operation to Abigail?"

"Not yet. I don't want her to know I'm just a guy slaving over a hot furnace. Two actually. She's asked me a lot about the process, and I told her some."

"You know what? You are nuts. You guys are perfect for each other."

"We are?" Now he looked like he was twelve.

"Well, you're having great sex, right?"

"Right."

"And she is an academic. And you have an academic brain. You don't have to go to school to have that kind of brain. You're like Bob Dylan."

"I am?" he took a big swig of beer. "Is that good?" he said. I could see he was starting to feel better. His eyes were bright and his cheeks were pink.

"Yeah," I said. "Young Bob had the mind of a rabbi. He could have been a Talmudic scholar. An amazing steel trap mind for detail and nuance, that could hold thousands of stories—word for word—and keep them straight. But he fell in love with old American music. So he applied that masterful brain to folk and blues, till he was a walking bible of arcane singers and songs. That's part of why his own songs go so deep."

"You have to go back to the originals," Jerome said.

"Does Abigail tell you about her work?" I said.

"Yeah, it's pretty cool. She's doing a thing now, trying to figure out how far sexual behavior reflects the power structure in society, as between men and women. She says they're not always parallel. I think she's onto something."

I nodded.

He made a sort of what-can-you-do gesture with his hands. Then he gave me a high-beam smile, stood up, and took out his cell phone.

"Tell her hello for me," I said.

19

not ready for prime time

$\mathcal{W}$e move now to Scenario B: where you and your partner *weren't* wrong for each other. You were basically a good match. This is the toughest case, because you really had a chance. You were, or had the potential to be, soulmates. Yet it still didn't work out. How sad is that? It's the most heartbreaking scenario, because instead of being unmasked as wrong for each other, the two of you linger in each other's minds, ghosts of what might have been.

As I said earlier, if you were in this situation in your last relationship, you are going to face the same challenge next time around. Because if things go right, you are again going to find a person who is a good match for you; only you'll want the result to be different.

If, on the other hand, you've decided during previous chapters that you were in Scenario A in your last relationship (incompatible partners), I would still hope that you are going to find a good match next time, somebody with whom you have the things in common that were lacking before.

For starters, we wash the car, rearrange the apartment, and buy a new jacket.

In *either* case, you are going to be trying to avoid Scenario B, where a good match goes wrong, and get to what we might call Scenario C: where you are well-matched with your partner *and* it works out right.

To do that, we need to understand some of the ways that a compatible couple can miss out on success. That's the topic of this chapter and the next. In this one, I want to look at the situation where the right person came along, but it was *too soon*. One or both partners weren't quite ready. How does that happen, and what can we learn from it?

When you meet a worthy mate, you have more motive to be the person you hadn't quite got around to being. You want your look, your weight, your health, your fitness, your home, your friends, your career, your dreams, your sexuality, your car—everything that can reflect on you—to reflect the real you, the best you.

So you look around at your life, and if some of these things don't exude the ideal you, it's a problem. What do you do, tell your new *amour* that they're going to have to postpone for a year or two so you can become the person you want them to see; or do you jump in?

Most of us jump in. Then, as fast as we can, we try to bring ourselves to a new level. For starters, we wash the car, rearrange the apartment, and buy a new jacket.

And all this is good. It's like preparing for a royal visit, or a stint on a reality show.

But sometimes it isn't enough. There are things you can't fix that quickly. Let's look at some of them.

career dreams

Many of us get so caught up in surviving that we put our career dreams on hold. We are in a sort of limbo; we tell ourselves that some day we'll break loose and do what we really want to do with our lives. But it's hard to make that escape.

The problem is that surviving has its own momentum. The job you're in makes demands, and you want to do well at it, even though it's not the one you aspire to. You start to have a little seniority. You need the benefits and you like some of the other employees. What you really want to do is to go back to school and qualify for the career that would fulfill you—or save enough money to take some time off and do your own thing—whatever it is, it would require an interruption of life as you know it.

You're much more likely to end up with someone you admire if you are working towards goals you think are admirable.

Then you meet someone and you join that life to theirs. The two of you should be in paradise together. Only your soul is in limbo.

The wrong job can certainly test a relationship. For one thing there's the misery factor. The more unhappy you are in your job, the more that spills over into the time you should be laughing, singing, dancing. There are two possibilities:

1. Your partner has their career together. Then there is this unpleasant contrast.

2. Your partner is unhappy too. That is a recipe for mutual slippage into a life of escapism. (Escapism is what people do when they can't escape.)

The solution would be to yank yourself out of limbo. Go to school, start your business, whatever. But you can't always turn the ship on a dime. And these endeavors are costly and risky. When you're starting life with a new person, you need stability, not racking upheaval. And you often need extra money.

But the biggest problem is not that miserable job. It's that *dream*. The one that's on hold. You and your partner may not be able to co-exist with it. Bad things happen to dreams that aren't happening. They get bloated; they lose muscle mass; they turn funny colors. They need a whole room just to house them. They don't go out much. They consume alcohol and they want other drugs. They start fights, because they don't like being ignored but it's hard to notice something that isn't happening. They interfere in every calculation, every planning session. "No, I can't move to that city where you've been offered a promotion, because my dream wouldn't like the climate there." "No, we can't have children because we don't have enough room for them *and* my dream."

With or without a stowaway dream, some people's circumstances just aren't ready for a voyage on the open seas. Woody Allen said that love is like a shark—it has to keep moving or it dies; and when the moment is right to buy a house or have kids or move to the next level in some other way, the moment has to be seized. If too many pieces aren't in place, the chance will be lost and then may come the bogging down into atrophy.

On the other hand, if two people are building something—if they have a mutual vision of where they're trying to go and if they are making headway in that direction—it matters not how far they are from the goal, especially if they're young. What is harder to handle is being mired in a position you don't want to be in, and not making any progress away from it.

Look back on your last relationship. Do you think: "We were soulmates but we just didn't have our paths together, and it dragged us down?"

That kind of thing can change. You take a look around when you're on your own, and spurred perhaps by a love that almost made it, you can decide it's time to really wake up to the neglected parts of your true self. So you open the curtains and start the next act of your life.

And even if that isn't the motive, you're much more likely to end up with someone you admire if you are working towards goals you think are admirable.

> The inability to deal with emotions is not a guy characteristic: it's an *immature guy* characteristic.

And sometimes, crazily, the person you meet farther down the road might even be the one you left behind. You weren't ready for each other then, but now the passage of time has cured the impasses that beset your respective life-plans. Other things may have been cured too; and the voyage may be back on . . .

Not having your life plan in good enough shape is one way that a person can be unready for serious couplehood. There are others.

immaturity

When two people are equally immature, that can fly. They can grow together. But there are so many departments. Sex, social life, emotional development, career, finances, work ethic, reliability, willingness to commit . . . And something that used to be called prudence: the ability to anticipate the risks in big and small situations, and thereby stave off disasters. If there is enough of a trade-off in different areas, if one person is more socially mature but the other is more financially mature, maybe the two can bring each other along. But too often there is a consistent pattern where one member of the couple is ahead of the other. That spells trouble, as you will no doubt recognize if you see this in your own past.

Oddly, many TV sitcoms seem to *endorse* this kind of discrepancy. We get a "man" who is really just an overgrown boy—sometimes literally overgrown, as on *The King of Queens*—and he is being carried by his spouse or girlfriend, who is slim, perky, long-suffering, and seems to have every aspect of her life together except the choice of her spouse. Many of these shows seem not to be about a husband and wife, but a man-child and his mother: the extreme case being *Everybody Loves Raymond*, where Ray seemed to have two mothers, one of whom he was married to.

In television comedies (and Judd Apatow movies) the immature male has the saving graces that he is loveable, gets laughs, and his faults are written off as the essence of guy-ness. In real life he may not fare so well. One example: the inability to deal with emotions is not a guy characteristic; it's an *immature guy* characteristic.

no vacancy: bart and annie

Bart and Annie found themselves on road trips together quite often, because of their insurance sales jobs. Both were divorced and looking, and both saw something they liked on the other side of the car seat. Annie was willowy, 42, with fine features; Bart was a weight lifter, 45, with a well-trimmed beard and good cheekbones. They quickly discovered a talent for mutual flirtation, a playfulness that made the occasional no-sales seem hilarious instead of depressing, and a yen for each other's bodies.

After a day of driving and talking to rural clients, our policy people often found themselves near the same sloppy Mexican restaurant on the outskirts of town, round about happy hour. A few margaritas got them moving briskly around the bases. One night they elected to stay in a motel instead of driving back to the office, and that was so much fun that they did it again, and again. Bart would wake up in the middle of the night to find Annie gone, but that added a hint of mystery. There was only one thing that bothered him about her: her feet smelled funny. When he was removing her shoes, a strong odor hit him, that he had to ignore. He wrote it off as a foot malady.

So it happened that Bart and Annie fell in love, on a sort of advance honeymoon, without ever having visited each other's places of abode.

Then one evening Bart went to Annie's for dinner. He found her house in a new development, in a maze of streets that all began with "Pinegrove". He knocked on the door and there was a giant brouhaha, a clamor of barking. Annie let him in and he was mowed down by three dogs—a German shepherd and two schnauzers—whose agenda was mostly friendly. When he got up again and walked into the carpeted living room, Bart had a moment of recognition. That smell, that he knew from her feet. It was everywhere. It was the dogs.

He sat on the couch and it was there. He went to the bathroom and it was there. The carpet was wall-to-wall, and it was in the carpet. That night in bed, not only was the smell there but so were the three dogs. Apparently this was where they slept, the shepherd by Annie's feet, the schnauzers near her head.

This minor point turned out to be a major stumbling block. Bart had nothing against dogs, and there was a beloved hound in his small-town past, but now as an adult city dweller he would have felt *one* dog to be a pretty big challenge, and would have wanted it to be well trained and mostly outside.

He tried to hint to Annie that it would be nice if they could sometimes be in the bedroom without the dogs, and she was, in her easygoing way, glad to shoo them out, but that created more of a canine distraction than having them in. The truth was that Annie was not willing to do anything that in any way lessened her closeness with her dogs. She could not and would not push them away.

Bart had a sensitive nose, and scents were a major erotic trigger for him. He loved the smell of Annie's perfume, and her hair, and her skin. He just couldn't enjoy them anymore because the aroma of dog was too loud.

Bart's torch for Annie began to flicker, and their sex life began to pall. One night he got her to stay at his place and he was able to recapture what it had been like—so delicious, so rich, so deep. So quiet. But she was distracted by the thought of her "boys" and left at two in the morning.

"You're not ready for a relationship with me," Bart said.

"But you're the one I want. You're the first man I've loved in twenty years."

"And I want you."

On the day he said goodbye, Bart really felt that Annie was his soulmate. Too bad she already had enough males in her life.

There are a number of ways that a person's lifestyle can render them unready to accommodate a serious mate. People can be at a point where their private way of life leaves no room for another. This can be true of anyone, at any age, who has structured their environment, or their habits, or their thoughts and feelings, in such a way that another, different person can't fit in.

They haven't left a vacancy in their life.

the shadow of the past

I want now to look at the most important possible explanation of Scenario B.

It will bring us full circle.

You still believe that in the marrow of your beings, you and your partner matched. So why couldn't you make a go of it?

The cause may have been that you hadn't done the very work we are trying to do in this book—with the relationships that came *before* that. Our whole effort has been to deal with the damage and unlock the lessons of the past, so it can't cripple the future. And the possibility we come across now, is that your last relationship was crippled by *the pasts that you or your partner carried into it.*

The original source of a lot of lovers' problems is a bad match somewhere back along the line.

The reason it didn't succeed, even though you were basically a good match, may be that you were too damaged by some *previous* relationship that hadn't been dealt with and therefore hadn't released you from its clutches.

If anything could prove that we need to do the work we're doing now, it would be that.

Any of the topics we have covered, any of the ways that a failed relationship can mar one's ability to love again, may already have applied to you or your partner before you even got going with each other.

- Maybe your partner was in the grip of a wounded ego from a previous breakup and couldn't really love you.

- Maybe you were in the control of rebound logic, inflicting a former lover's mistakes on the new one.

- Maybe one of you was the victim of previous cheating, and arrived with trust/power issues that sank the ship.

- Maybe one of you was so mired in a fallen world that you couldn't get out.

- Maybe you or he carried false lessons out of a previous relationship, which made you feel like a failure.

If so, now is the time to shine a light on that former damage and deal with it once and for all. As I suggested in the Introduction, look at the last relationship, but use it also as a window on others farther back, that you recognize as still having negative power over you. Probably you have already been doing this: when we surveyed the toxic legacies of failed *amour*, your mind likely leapt to *whichever* past loves most affect you today.

There's another striking point to make here. The earlier relationship that made you unready for the *good* match may well have been a *bad* match—the kind we studied under Scenario A. In other words, when you look at a person's history you often find they were with the wrong person farther back in the past, and that managed to poison the ground later with someone who could have been right. The original source of a lot of lovers' problems is a bad match somewhere back along the line. This is because, as we saw in our incompatibility clinic, people so often draw the wrong conclusions from mismatches. They carry forward a sense of inadequacy or failure that they have incorrectly gleaned from the simple fact of having been with the wrong partner.

If this happened to you, it is time now to stop the cycle—to make sure you will no longer carry on the effects of that older relationship. Turn your attention to it, sort out the ways in which it was a case of incompatibility, and exonerate yourself of the false charges that you may have been dragging along with you.

And know this: even after you've dissected a mismatch and defanged its allegations, there may still be some lingering insecurities. That's what mismatches do. They make us think we are lacking in whatever areas went badly. (And that's why it's so important to avoid them.) We become insecure in areas where we have failed, even if the reason for the failure was incompatibility, not any flaw of our own. A small voice inside us says, *maybe it'll always be that way for me*. The ultimate cure is to do better in that very arena, in real time. It's kind of like a fighter who has lost a big bout. He may study the tape and train like a maniac and spar for long hours, but until he steps back in the ring and things go better, there will be a shadow of a doubt.

So you're going to need to have positive experiences with your next partner, to heal any insecurities that you bring to the table. How to do this? There are two essential steps. One is to admit the insecurity to yourself, by going through a process like the one we've traveled. The second is to tell your new partner about it when you feel it. Tell them, "I get a little uptight in this kind of situation, because I was in a relationship where it didn't go so well." If you find the right person, they will have no trouble dealing with this kind of admission. In fact they will welcome it, love you for being so honest, and try to help you find your way again.

I'm taking a walk on a cliff overlooking the river when I see an older woman who is painting a watercolor. She has hazel eyes and gray hair under a straw hat. She is in a wheelchair. We strike up a conversation and she pours me a glass of lemonade. I tell her I'm working on a book. She asks me what topic I'm writing about and I say, the ways in which compatible people can go off the rails, by not being ready for a relationship.

She smiles at me in a wistful way and says, "There are things a couple *can't* be ready for. Even if they're ready for each other."

I look at her, wondering what hard-won wisdom life has thrown her way. "That's interesting," I say carefully.

"Calamities," she says. "Acts of God, they're sometimes called."

"I see what you mean."

"Do you? There aren't any guarantees, you know. People can have it all, and it can be taken away from them. And it isn't their fault."

"Like the loss of a child," I say. "That can tear the parents apart."

"I had a man once," she says. "He loved me, and I loved him. We were really good together."

I feel a shiver in my scalp. *We're talking about this wheelchair,* I think to myself.

"Something happened," I say. That sounds awkward and trite, and I add, "I'm sorry."

She touches my hand and smiles at me. "It's okay," she says. "I've had a while to deal with it. Forty years. All I'm saying is, I don't blame him that it fell apart. And I don't blame me."

"Was it . . . "

"In our case, it came down to the guilt," she says. "We were in a car. He was behind the wheel. It was after a concert—Vivaldi, very good. We had a silly disagreement about whether to go home or to a late-night restaurant. He won. We moved on a green light and we were hit on the passenger side."

"That's terrible."

"It was a drunk driver. We were twenty-five. I didn't have to forgive my guy, because it wasn't his fault. But he begged me to. So I said I did. But that didn't help, because he couldn't forgive himself. He couldn't look at me. He saw the woman he had crippled."

A man her age walks up and rests his hands on the back of the wheelchair in an unhurried way. She reaches back and touches his hand. "We just couldn't get past it," she says, and begins to pack up her paints.

So that's a good thing to bear in mind. The painter lady said it: sometimes life throws something at a couple that they just *can't* be ready for. No amount of advice or preparation is going to make them equal to it.

That can give us perspective, though. It reminds us that it's a tough world, and if you again find yourself with a good person, and the two of you have a chance to make it work, you want to do everything you can to make that come true.

20

how good matches go wrong

and how to do better next time

$\mathcal{I}$n this chapter we reach the last, but not the least, stage in our journey. We have looked at ways that you or your partner may have been unready for a major relationship, even though you were a good match. But what if you *were* ready in those respects? How did it go wrong?

We're now getting down to avoidable mistakes, the kind that make you lie in bed at four in the morning thinking, "I blew it with that person; I could have done better. Because the time was right; all the pieces were in place." This is where we look at things that were in your power to change. And the reason they are so worth looking at is exactly that. You can change them next time. A little more alertness,

She got up on the big morning to find Gordon working on an oyster-and-cornbread stuffing.

effort, courage, or simple caring can save the day. So each of the following reasons why things go wrong will transform into a positive recommendation.

the trouble with happiness

Sophie loved the holidays. She was very good at finding funny, imaginative gifts and putting together a classic turkey dinner. True, she usually ended up doing all the work when her family got together, but she had accepted that.

The first year that she and Gordon lived together in Durango, they decided they would have Christmas with just the two of them, and she was assuming she would play her usual role. But Gordon said, "You made Thanksgiving dinner for ten people, so let me do Christmas." Sophie said sure, not quite believing her ears.

She got up on the big morning to find Gordon working on an oyster-and-cornbread stuffing, with a sizable bird sitting in the sink. She flitted around him, making teasing comments, and he shooed her away, but not before she said under her breath, "We usually have the regular bread stuffing."

He took a break and they opened presents. He was astonished by the linen shirt she had bought him—he said nobody ever got him shirts he liked—and loved the edition of Shakespeare with the good footnotes. But she too had her moment to be astonished: he had found century-old postcards of her hometown in Illinois, one of them showing the municipal building where her grandfather had worked. And he had gotten her a nice sweater that fit perfectly and showed off her green eyes. As she sat on the couch, a strange feeling came over her, that this was just too perfect, like something in a movie. She felt that Gordon was nice, and she was nice, and the perfect sunny weather was nice, and it was all a little too nice to take. For a moment she couldn't imagine having sex with him, because he seemed too angelic in his robin's egg blue T-shirt and charcoal sweat pants. She made a snide comment about how maybe he should buy *all* her clothes for her. He looked confused and she left the room.

He followed her into the bedroom and asked her what was wrong. She said, "The holidays always make me blue. I'll be okay." But it wasn't true; the holidays never made her blue.

Dinner was interesting and tasty; Gordon had done a great job. As he opened the wine he'd chosen, he said, "This is supposed to be a non-oaky chardonnay, very different. We'll see if the wine guy lied to me." He poured a little in her glass.

Sophie tasted it and it *was* non-oaky, and that was a cool thing, but somehow it set her off. Through the wine glass she saw the cranberries in a bowl. "I really don't like jellied cranberry," she said in a tone whose bitterness surprised even her.

"Honey, I'm sorry, I should have known that," Gordon said, and his sweet reasonableness incensed her.

She said, "I've had enough of this," and went out the door to the backyard, where a gentle snow was starting to fall.

She stood out there, wanting a cigarette for the first time in years, her brain buzzing. Why was she *being* this way? What on earth was the matter with her?

Then it hit her. She had just been terrified, all day, of this new experience. She wasn't in her traditional comfort zone, slinging food for the whole company, doing all the giving and not getting much in return. She was afraid that this perfect symmetry of her and Gordon both giving to each other was somehow unreal, that it would melt like a projected color slide.

The very things she loved most about Gordon, his creativity and energy, his generosity, were making her nervous, as if she might not be equal to them.

She was being threatened by the very things that had made her fall in love with him! This was ridiculous. She started to weep and laugh at the same time. Then she felt his arm around her and she leaned her head on his chest.

"I'm nuts," she said. "I'm just nuts. This has been wonderful." She kissed him and it felt just as sexy as when mortals kiss. They were safe; not angels yet, after all.

Sometimes happiness itself is the hurdle you can't get over. If you've been in the heart's wilderness and then good news comes along, it could just throw you for a loop. You find yourself for the first time in your life joined to someone you could really get along with, and that can make a person uneasy. You aren't used to it. Maybe it won't last. Maybe it feels implausible, or even corny.

Maybe it makes you nervous because it would be so great if it turned out to be real. The stakes are so high; there is so much to lose. A sort of performance anxiety sets in, like that of an Olympic gymnast who has done this maneuver a hundred times before, but now is shaky because this one is for the medal.

Fear sets in. So you do something to muck the situation up. That way the tension is broken and the fear of falling relieved (you can't fall if you're already on the ground). Some demon within makes you behave badly, so you can return to the ordinary, a more comfortable place to be.

Fear is a slippery emotion, because it conceals itself from us just at the moment that it grips us. It likes to work incognito, to be the invisible puppeteer. It packs a sort of double-whammy: it makes us hide, not only from the external thing that scares us, but also from the fact that we are afraid. The trick, therefore, is to detect when you are scared, call the knave by his name and not allow him to transfer his force in some other direction, like spite or malice, mischief or flight.

So if, in your next relationship, you find yourself about to tip the boat, stop and figure out why. If the answer is fear, fight it directly, don't fight the relationship.

setting the bar too high

In answer to skepticism about lasting love, we sometimes hear people say, "My grandparents are still madly in love after fifty years of marriage." For some reason, this kind of thing is less often reported about one's parents.

Maybe the lesson here is that grandparents have had enough time to set their expectations realistically. They are wise enough to be pleased by a lot of things: still being alive, still having the ability to go for a walk and read a book. And still having each other. The rest of us should be so smart.

transferring discontent

There are bound to be a lot of times when you are dissatisfied with life. The weather is drizzly; your favorite politician is being slandered; home prices are falling; gas prices are too high; the corn flakes taste bland; and your hair looks thin in the mirror.

A deep human instinct tells us that the best relief from the defects in our own existence is to find flaws in another person. And the opportunity is enhanced if that someone is close, is known in lavish detail, and relies on our support. Most people have some sensitive areas, and no one detects them better than a spouse. So we slip into the habit of critiquing each other. It can be dangerous.

I talked in Chapter 15 about avoiding a partner whose tastes you just don't appeal to. It's like installing a derogatory critic in your life. Definitely a bad idea. But no one is perfect. Even when two people basically dig each other, there are going to be areas that one could find fault with if one wanted to try.

Most people are their own worst critics; they don't need any help. So a good rule of thumb is not to lend a hand.

don't pick on things a person can't change

Most good people are conscious of their flaws, both physical and mental, and are hoping to be deemed acceptable in spite of them. They may even dream that their mate doesn't notice these blemishes, or thinks they are unimportant. The thing is, if you say something, you can't take it back. If you tell your lover that you find his tenor voice annoying, or that his lack of articulateness irks you, then he is stuck with these news items. And the announcement may well cause them to get worse.

how about things a person *can* change?

This target isn't much better. That's because most of us are already working on the areas where we know we could improve; or if we aren't, we want to be.

What is even better is being loved later on.

Ryan was a light smoker who wanted to quit. He got a sinus infection and was on an antibiotic for a week, and for several days he couldn't bring himself to consume any cigarettes. His wife Barbara decided this opportunity needed seizing, and elected to take the lead in this noble cause. So she said, "Honey, you only have one pack in your possession. You're already three days into quitting; you're practically there! This smoking thing is a deal-breaker for me. So give me the pack and I'll get rid of it." Ryan couldn't find a way to say no to this; it made perfect sense.

Ryan was also facing a stressful time at work. This sudden onset of not smoking aggravated that stress and caused him to turn to snacking as a refuge. Three weeks later he started sneaking cigarettes again, but now he had gained ten pounds, was near a meltdown, and was lying to his spouse. In every way he was farther back than he had been before Barbara imposed her improvement agenda on him.

For most of us, it is much harder to climb that mountain if our spouse makes it their idea, or makes their love contingent on our doing it.

The take-away

If you feel discontented sometimes, don't inflict it on your partner; try to deal with your own issues directly, and maybe even ask them for their help.

That way, you protect a precious thing. During the first enchantment of being in love, we tend to idealize our partners above all others and see them as perfect. That's nice for them, being adored at that stage when we don't know them so well, but what is even better is being loved later on, when we know them through and through—faults and all. The pledge of that first infatuation is redeemed when your partner finds that they are loved in that more informed way.

And a little restraint can help convey the good news.

reining in conflict

When two people basically like and love each other, the last thing they would want, or even believe possible, is that they could become enemies. That's why it's very important to keep the reins on hostility.

Once loosed in the room, hostility can sometimes feed on itself. It's as if it comes with its own escalation pill. It goes ahead and takes over the script, writes lines that are meaner and more injurious than the two people really mean. But then they have to back up those lines.

So it's better not to let it start.

Conflict is bound to arise in a relationship. Life is too complicated for everybody to get every decision right the first time. Somebody will get it wrong, and the other person may see that, and there it is: disagreement. Or there is no right answer, just two different preferences, and both can't be accommodated.

But disagreements can be resolved without getting hostile. We can have an open discussion or even a spirited debate, and we can listen to each other and find common ground. Here are three good ways to resist the lure of hostility:

- Don't get mad at the other person for disagreeing with you. As if they have no right. They do have a right!

- Don't let cowardice lead the way, by being afraid you'll *lose* if you submit to a calm discussion, and getting angry in advance over that imagined outcome. Better to be brave and say your piece.

- If you secretly think you're wrong, don't blame your partner for that. Admit it.

If a couple follows these (hard-earned) suggestions, they'll never get to the next stages of the process, which (if memory serves) may witness such ploys as fighting dirty, taking unfair advantage, and using volume or manipulation to try to find a shortcut to victory. Or doing what political ads do nowadays—attacking the person instead of the position they're taking.

The rule of karma applies here, and it applies to the *couple*. Every time two people let themselves slip into hostility and viciousness, it becomes easier for them to make that transition (equals harder not to) the *next* time they encounter conflict. The story of Dr. Jekyll and Mr. Hyde contains the same lesson: every time the good Jekyll took the potion that made him turn into the bad Hyde, it made the leap easier in the future. Until by the end, Jekyll was changing into Hyde *without* taking the potion, and he couldn't get back to his good self because there was no more of the chemical available. So a couple can watch their good self

recede into history, no longer reachable because they have betrayed it too often.

Such a tragedy can be avoided with a little courage, a little compassion, and a steely desire to maintain civility. That can get a couple
through rough times without damage to the warmth that they'll need
when times get better.

frivolous straying

Very often, the way that two well-matched people end up apart is
that one of them falls in love with somebody else, and by the time
that peters out, it's too late to go back. We've already seen a glaring
instance of this: Cassie's affair with the unkind pianist Matt, which
nearly ended her chances with the excellent Bill.

**Picture life without your
partner, before you slip out
the back door.**

You don't miss your water till your
well runs dry. But a good rule of thumb
here is try, try very hard, to imagine
being without your water while the
well is still flowing. Picture life with-
out your partner, before you slip out the back door. Think what it
would be like not to have access to them anymore.

Excitement is alluring. It can make mere contentment seem like
a trifle. But as we have seen, the thrill of falling in love is often fueled
by the very unsuitability of the object.

Long shots are fun to bet on, but they have this nasty habit of
not coming in.

So those blah times that couples go through are dangerous. They
make you restless, make you think you have to do something rash.
Better to do something for the couple you're already in: ask your partner out on a real date; do something racy and different with them;
invite some people over that bring out the best in the two of you;
apply yourself to some task that your partner cares about.

the big chance

A kind of pall can fall over a couple if they pass up a big life opportunity out of caution, or even worse, out of lack of faith in the couple.

It can be very hard to live with someone who put on the brakes at the one moment when all the resources were there and the signs were right. The moment may never come again, but the chance to think about it will remain.

So when a big chance comes along, don't give it a no vote on some automatic, superficial ground. Take a real look at it and make sure you're finding out what your partner really feels: how much of their heart is invested in it. And hopefully they will do the same for you. Even when a courageous move doesn't work out, there's the bond forged by the fact that the two of you were willing to try. Sometimes you just have to say, "Let's go for it."

attention deficit and contact surplus

If you miss enough episodes of a series with an ongoing plot, you may not be able to engage with it anymore.

That's true of relationships too. Partners can drift apart because they forget to tune in on each other's inner story. In our world, time is such a threatened commodity that a couple may have only cursory conversation on a typical weekday. A quick check-in and a short exchange of facts. That isn't enough to keep the fire burning.

If, after some years together, your spouse no longer took the time to draw out your thoughts, you may have developed a gagged sensation, as if your microphone had been shut off and your voice wasn't wanted. Those empty moments, when you had something heartfelt to say and your partner skidded right past it—did they eventually make you want to leave the venue?

You may have developed a gagged sensation, as if your microphone had been shut off.

We need to find out what our mate wants to talk about today—not what we want to hear about. And when your partner tries to talk to you about something that wasn't on your radar screen, make time for it. Don't present yourself as available for conversation if you aren't. Don't ask a cursory question and then tune out. Don't always be doing something else while your main squeeze is talking. And don't let any of this be done to you by someone you love.

Not enough attention is one thing; too much contact is another. For most of us there is a cycle of needing company and needing solitude. It is fatiguing to constantly be monitored by another human being, even one you love. So don't forget that on occasion, the best gift you can give your partner is to be unaware of him. Go out, get scarce.

We are very forgiving of our friends. We show our fine ability to get along with others by not expecting any one friend to be all things to us. That's a nice favor to extend to one's spouse, too.

Finally, don't resent your poor partner for knowing you. That's what keeps you from being alone.

television: the nemesis across the room

In the evening, two people sat down on a couch feeling friendly and close.

Three hours later they got up to go to bed, feeling completely alienated from each other.

What happened? They watched a television.

Most of us agree that TV is harmful to children, and their hours should be limited and controlled. But we pretend that at some magic age that stops being true. I disagree: I think it's bad for adults too. And I especially think that it can be bad for couples who watch together.

I'm not talking about when you and your mate rent a great movie or watch a program you both like. The more selective you are, and the more control you have over commercials, the closer to benign TV is. And today's DVR's, TIVO, and on-demand can do a lot to put you in charge.

You acknowledge the performers, but they rudely ignore you.

No, I'm talking about when you and your mate expose yourselves to the raw world of television, and especially when one of you has the remote in hand and you share the bizarre experience we call channel-surfing. (Which is never really shared. The one holding the remote control cannot possibly make the same moment-to-moment choices that the other would make—so the mutuality is an illusion.)

I have to admit I have a personal vendetta here that I need to get off my chest. But I think I'm really onto something that affects couples, a toxin that can slip too easily into our shared lives. So if you bear with me about the nefarious things that TV does to us, I think it will have a payoff about relationships.

a rant only a tv-addict could have written

A television is a weird animal. Because we are so used to it, we have forgotten what an intruder it is in the room. Because it is visual and auditory and moving, TV triggers social reflexes in us in a way that, for example, reading doesn't. As far as your nervous system is concerned, the people on the screen are in the room with you, and so are the people laughing on the phony laugh track. I've actually been embarrassed by my partner walking in the room and catching me grinning at Jay Leno and his guest as if I was on the set with them!

The problem is, it's unilateral. You acknowledge the performers, but they rudely ignore you. And when they do things that should be private—as increasingly happens these days—TV doesn't worry about sparing your feelings, any more than a too-thin motel wall would.

It's as if a bunch of people you don't know were to camp in your living room and carry on, not in any way concerned that you are sitting there. TV bombards you with other people's worlds—*their* victories, *their* supposed glamour, *their* moment-to-moment choices. By doing so it invalidates you. Since you aren't on the screen, you don't exist.

But wait, that's not all! You also get the following invasions of your dignity:

- TV tells you that how you look, and whether you manage not to look old, is the most important thing about you: and it dictates what the "correct" way to look is. In every area—body, face, teeth, eyes, wardrobe, weight, shape—it's on your case.

- TV tries all the time to make you feel inadequate. It says: "You aren't young enough; you aren't famous enough; not rich enough; not good enough at what you do. You aren't the best because if you were, you'd be on the screen with us. You aren't having enough fun. Look at us cavorting, grinning, laughing people, and you just sitting on a couch."

- TV tries to scare you. It says, "We have just discovered a new disease that you probably have; notice how familiar the symptoms sound; you're going to die if you don't buy this new drug."

- TV isolates each spectator from the others, because each of us is sensitive to different things. It makes you feel alone, afraid of being found out as too hurt or too turned on. So it has an inherent separating force. When a man and a woman watch together, the woman may feel upstaged by the female flesh running rampant on the screen, and the man may feel caught somewhere between voyeurism and cheating. Half the time we watch things we half-hate; but when someone else is there, they may not catch this nuance.

- TV is ADD gone wild. Not only do endless ads interrupt programs, but programs interrupt themselves with little animated figures advertising *other* programs. No wonder so many of us have ADD, especially those raised by television sets. Our hard drives get regularly defragmented, but it's our brains that really need it.

- TV is soaked in the logic of the ego. It used to be that people who were famous only for being famous were laughed at, but now they're honored as much as those who earned their fame by actually doing something. Pundits always rave about whether some politician's statement is a *winner*, not whether it's true. People who cheat and lie are admired if they get what they want. Television is like a goad to the toad inside you. If you watch enough of it, your heart starts to atrophy.

Commercials are the worst. They take the highest artistic skills and prostitute them. Much of the time, they deceive. They have to, because their product doesn't really do what they say it does, whether that product is a drug or a soft drink or a politician.

During commercials, you and your true love are sitting silently, being forced to watch a stream of lies. It's almost like a form of humiliation.

No wonder you may rise up after a few hours of this, feeling cut off from your own self and estranged from your partner. Couples should protect themselves against this influence. In fact, free-range television—by which I mean channel-surfing—is so personal a form of intercourse with such a sticky entity, that it may be better practiced alone. When you surf with someone else, the cognitive dissonance between you builds up and becomes more awful with every choice that the other person wouldn't have made, and every flickering image that you aren't seeing the same way.

Okay. Rant over. Thank you for listening.

As I suggested earlier, there are ways to avoid the worst of TV's impositions. There *are* wonderful things to watch, and most of them are available in a commercial-free form, at a time chosen by you, not them. When you're building a relationship as a couple, make a habit from the start of doing other things besides TV. Be conscious about what television offerings you choose to share, and later on, make sure that the tube doesn't creep into a position it doesn't deserve.

the opposite of sex

Between two people who love each other, good sex not only provides hours of enjoyment in itself, but it does a whole lot to keep other things spinning along.

- It helps keep the romance alive. It's more than natural to hold hands across a table in a nice restaurant if you had orgasms together the night before.

- It gives you a break from the ceaseless grind of logistics that is modern life, makes time stop.

- It encourages emotional openness, closeness and forgiveness.

- It alleviates the natural irritation of living in close quarters with another human being.

- It avoids the problem of not having sex.

- It's good for your self-esteem, and your sense of your own attractiveness.

- It's good for your health.

- It cures at least one kind of frustration, thus making others easier to bear.

- It makes you feel so young.

And the list goes on.

So if good sex turned into no sex in your last relationship, you may not be wrong in counting that as a real factor in sinking the alliance.

Which raises the question, how do two people who once had enjoyable sex end up not having any?

Well, it could be that:

1. they weren't really sexually compatible, and after some time together, that fact emerged;

2. they were sexually compatible, but they never took the trouble to learn each other properly;

3. they had it goin' on big time, but they let it slip away;

4. the relationship went so sour that it killed the sex;

5. the years took it away.

Factors 1 and 4 may not be that easy to deal with other than by finding a better-matched partner, but the rest deserve some discussion. In fact they go together.

As people get older (especially men), it may take a little more to start them up; at least Mick Jagger said that in a song. And as two people who are running a household become overly familiar with each other, wearing every possible hat other than "Sensual Being," that spark of mystery can easily fade. People get into habits that are less than sexy. Everything is about getting through a To Do list, including the last thing on that list, falling into bed exhausted.

That's why it can be an advantage if, in the days when sex is the path of least resistance, you and your partner take the time to explore each other's fantasies and find each other's happy buttons. This sort of expertise can come in very handy later on, when sex becomes a little less inevitable.

Ironically, when people are courting and they have the excitement of newness (and often youth) on their side, they seem to make much more effort to present themselves as glamorous and seductive, than they do later on when this kind of help may be more sorely needed.

The early evening, every day, was a *date*.

Long ago in the twentieth century, I remember a strange custom that I witnessed in the older generation. A man came home from work, dressed in a fine suit and tie (back then a lot of men had a relationship with someone called a tailor). Did he immediately cast off his duds and reappear in an undershirt and shorts? No, he stayed to pour a drink for his wife, who may have worn sloppy clothes during the day (more likely not) but who thought it a good idea to dress up for dinner. That's because the early evening, every day, was a *date*, and the kids were supposed to stay out of the way because there was adult bonding going on, and it was sexy and romantic—it was foreplay.

Now I would not want a return to those thrilling days when men were men and women had few choices for personal fulfillment. But there may be a lesson there for us moderns. Maybe we could remember to stimulate each other visually; maybe we could on occasion dress as nicely for our lover as we do for the corporations who exploit us. Maybe more evenings could be like dates.

Another good idea is to be aware of timing. If you know a time when you both tend to be most sexual, maybe that crucial window of opportunity should be honored as a good thing. And if you know an easy way to use wardrobe to get your partner hankering after you, why not go there unexpectedly? Men are so simple that it's a pity not to take advantage of them.

And finally, let us remember what a mystic once said. Even when sex is too high a mountain to climb, there's a meadow that's pretty easy to get to, where a lot of the same flowers grow: it's called cuddling.

how to get what you want

There are two possible approaches when your needs are not being met by your partner. The first one, which is very popular, is to sit and fume and get righteously indignant because after all, your partner should *know* what you want and should give it to you.

The second method requires a little humility and a tad of courage, but it has a major advantage: it works. *Ask your partner for what you want.*

keeping the faith

Life is like a canoe trip.

The morning may consist of taking down the tent in the rain; the afternoon may be a grueling slog against the wind, digging your paddle in until your arm is aching, in a fight against a lake that seems to go on forever. But then you get to the next campsite and you're sitting on a rocky point eating hot wieners and beans, and suddenly the whole past day looks brilliant, and you remember the way the sun glinted off the waves in the afternoon.

Life involves a lot of soldiering on, having faith that things will get festive again. And being with a great partner doesn't change that. The relationship itself will have routine stretches: there will be times when you can see no glamour and no glow to the other person, even though nothing very bad has happened. And then of course, something bad will happen.

But then . . . something good will. When it does, relish that moment together, celebrate it and allow it to radiate its charm back over the trek that got you there.

making loyalty stick

When you've done really well, see it through.

A woman's partner was floored by a life-threatening illness and she was utterly stricken by the thought of anything happening to him; so she waded into the situation and took care of him in every way, making sure the insurance was handled right and the hospital care was the best, staying at his bedside for long hours, fending off careless medical personnel, saving him from the wrong foods, protecting his job . . . and then he began to recover and finally, months later, he started to feel good again.

The moment of victory. Her partner thanked her and hugged her, but he felt so well, was so insouciant, that it seemed he didn't fully realize what danger he had been in, or what lengths she had gone to, to protect him. At this point a strange, tiny voice passed like a shadow through her mind, saying, "How can he be so carefree? Is he taking this for granted? How shall I punish the scoundrel?"

But then she caught herself and thought, *this is where I wanted him to be. Not even knowing how close he came to the abyss. I got him here and I am going to keep him here.*

Loyalty is so good if you make it last for the duration.

There is no greater blessing than having a partner who looks back at their past and is glad that you were in it, and conscious that you pulled them through some hard times (they may even know how hard). I don't mean that it's fun to bask in someone else's gratitude (although that's true). I mean that it's good to know that someone else has a positive view of the human heart, thinks it's something that can be counted on, because they can look back and know that when it really mattered, you came through.

the journey forward

$\mathcal{I}$ hope that when and if you are ready to try a new relationship, this book has helped you approach it with a fresh heart. And I hope you'll find a good partner to try with. Guidelines on how to do that are found in *Why Mr. Right Can't Find You*, and I've added more in this book, especially concerning how to detect mismatches and how to avoid plunging into them. I've also talked about the lessons of good matches that went wrong. But what I want to say now is that the journey we've been on is never done.

Finding your way with a new person who could be the one, is treacherous and thrilling and scary and delicate and it's real. While it's happening, life will throw new challenges your way, that you'll have to solve. And no matter how well you've dealt with the past, what's left of your demons will sometimes rise up and try to disrupt things. As I said before, the only way to convince them that you've won and they've lost is to beat them in real time.

It's good that you've cross-examined them and found the flaws in their claims. They are weakened now, but they will still try to do some mischief. The ego will try to interfere; rebound logic will rear its resentful head; fears and doubts will still surface. So you'll have to face them down under match conditions; you'll have to be alert enough to catch them at their tricks and vanquish them when it really matters. Including when they surface in your partner, who is after all, another person trying to be redeemed.

Part of that challenge, strange as it may sound, is fighting against incompatibility. There isn't always a hard line between differences that can be overcome and differences that spell deal-breaker. If you care about somebody, it's your job to stop small things from turning into big things. One cool way to do that, when you see a crevice that could turn into a chasm, is leap across it, to the other side. Find common ground by standing where your partner is standing. If they have a lonely interest, make it yours too. If there is a disagreement, concede the point; lose. Do it with sincerity, with all your heart. You won't believe the benefits that can bring. And the main one is, you'll win by losing: you'll score one as a soldier against discord. Another is, your partner may decide they can compromise on that very issue. Or they may just be so grateful that they'll concede something else that you *wouldn't* be able to give in on.

The rest of the challenge is to learn to step back when you sense trouble, and ask yourself, who is talking here? What old grudges are in play, old hurts stinging, false lessons echoing, that have nothing to do with two innocent people?

Two people who are on a new, unique, and enviable journey.

I hope the process we've gone through will help that journey happen.

epilogue

I walked down to the fruit stand on Saturday afternoon and bought an orange. I was standing there in the sun peeling it when I heard my name being called.

I turned and saw Bar Guy and Ms. Professor coming towards me. Abigail was looking very unprofessor-like in a T-shirt and shorts. Jerome seemed almost formal next to her, in a cream jacket over Chinos.

"We saw you go by," he said. "We're at the coffee shop. Join us."

As I strolled along between them, her hand on my arm and his on my shoulder, I felt like I was in some sort of romantic custody. We got to the café and they indicated a table on the sidewalk. They said they'd be back in a minute with drinks.

On one side of the table was a stack of academic journals; on the other a newspaper. I took a chair with no literature in front of it.

Abigail appeared with some mocha concoction and sat down in front of the newspaper. Then Jerome appeared with two beers and took the other chair.

"How have you been?" he said. "We've been talking about you."

"Oh, I've been writing."

"What's that like?"

"Torture?" Abigail said. She reached for Jerome's beer and took a swig.

"Not always," I said. "It's kind of like a canoe trip."

"I think I know what you mean," Abigail said. "And I don't even canoe."

I must have looked surprised.

"But explain, please," she added, giving me heightened attention.

I said, "That's okay. There's a more important topic. What have you two been saying about me?"

They looked at each other and hesitated. Then Jerome laughed. "I told her you influenced me at a crucial moment. So we have you to blame if this doesn't work out."

While he was saying that, he handed her the top journal in his stack. It had a red post-it sticking out.

"He's been reading articles for me," she said. "Making sure they're not relevant to my paper. But he keeps finding ones that are. Then I have to read them."

"I'm just a bad person," he said.

She handed him his beer and he snagged her hand in his. They both beamed at me.

"I should get him another beer," Ms. Professor told me. "I've almost finished his."

"I was wondering," Bar Guy said.

For some time I had been waiting for a chance to say, "How are things going with you two?"

But it didn't seem necessary.